Bulls-Eye Cover Letters
Table of Contents

This book is dedicated to the most important woman in the world, my wife Marisa and our lovely children, Colten, Arielle, Calais, Trinity and Rachel.

INTRODUCTION

This book attempts to demystify and define the proper use of the cover letter as one of the key elements of a successful job search. I use the term "demystify" because far too many people think that the idea of writing a concise, focused and compelling letter is a mystery, but it shouldn't be. Really the cover letter should be one of the easiest things you need to create to reach your dream job.

With that said, it doesn't mean that the cover letter can't be the star of the entire job search. Companies, like humans, tend to appreciate the fact that you admire them, that you know something salient about them and that you understand what makes them special. The problem is, if we use a staid, boring or un-interesting approach at wooing them, we can strike out just like the poor schmuck who uses cheesy pickup lines at the local club. In other words, we need to think differently and do things uniquely – that is why I wrote the book.

By the time you are done with chapter one, I promise you will never look at another cover letter in the same way you have come to see them now. I hope that you love what you read, apply what you learn and achieve the job that allows you to bloom as a professional.

CHAPTER 1

Use "Bulls-Eye" Cover Letters to Execute a Targeted Job Search

A Bulls-Eye cover letter is the answer to a question that every job seeker has, "How do I find a great job at a good company if my personal and professional network doesn't include someone that works at the target company I am interested in pursuing?" The answer is to use a "Targeted" cover letter.

Executing a strategic career search begins with a simple premise: To win a good job it's not always what you know, but quite often it's whom you know that really matters. To capture a great job, it's much easier to work from the top of the hiring chain than from the bottom, i.e., its better to personally know the CEO than the janitor. In the real world, wouldn't you agree that good jobs often go to friends of the captains of industry? The problem is, most of us don't know CEOs, corporate Presidents or HR managers personally, and so landing an offer at our target company remains a mystery to most job seekers. But there are simple techniques that can demystify a targeted job search.

Bulls-Eye Cover Letter Definition

Conducting company research online by reading press releases, newspaper articles, trade journal articles etc, that quote key decision makers, (those are also the hiring authorities such as senior executives at the target companies) and writing a cover letter to these decision makers that refer to the research you conducted and where you tell them you want to be part of the initiative, rollout or project that is touted in the article, press release or newsletter.

The research you need to conduct focuses on uncovering topical issues impacting the target company that you will leverage in order to turn a cold lead (someone we don't have a good reason to bother), into a warm lead (which is someone who becomes your internal champion) who is willing to refer you to a hiring manger or another link in the hiring chain.

If this is clear as mud to you, bear with me as I break it down.

Targeted career searching presupposes the following:

- That you pick target companies you want to work at – How many? There is no perfect answer, the more the merrier, but a good rule of thumb is 10-25 at a minimum.

- That you use the Internet or work with the Reference Librarian at your local library to learn how to use their online databases that contain the press releases and corporate information that is pertinent to the target companies where you want to work.

- That you have courage and tenacity to stick to the plan. Courage to believe you will be a valuable asset to the company you are targeting. And tenacity to stay with something that will pay off if you learn that people are accessible when you give them a justifiable reason to listen to you.

THE BULLS-EYE COVER LETTER MODEL

Question How do you find a job at a company where you have no contacts?
Answer   Use targeted career research as follows (read each step closely, with special attention in step 1 to use a reference librarian at your largest local library).

Three Key Actions

① Go to main library, *find a Business Reference Librarian* - ask him or her to help you locate the Online Business Databases and look for articles in a career area you are interested in targeting, i.e. sports marketing. Identify companies that specialize in your interest area.

   Example Sport Marketing job at IMG (world's largest sports marketing firm). Total research time = 15 minutes

② Look for new directions the company is taking (i.e. IMG buys Clear Channel's event marketing firm, Live Entertainment to form IMG Live!)
   - Get names of decision makers and send resumes to them. In this case they noted that Lee Heffernan will continue to manage the new IMG division. If you go to IMG Live! Website you will find Lee Heffernan's email address in the "who we are" section.

③ Write a cover letter that references something they were quoted as saying in the press release or article. Send resume and cover letter to target audience.

REAL CLIENT EXAMPLE 1: AMANDA GRAUL

Amanda was a recent college graduate with a degree in marketing and wanted to pursue a career in corporate event planning. Like many new college graduates, Amanda sent a resume and standard cover letter to a variety of potential employers. But Amanda had her eye on working at the Ice Palace, which happens to be the home of the Tampa Bay Lighting, a premier NHL hockey team. Of course, Amanda did not have contacts at the Ice Palace so the letter she wrote was generic in form and content.

9

Amanda Graul   *before cover letter*

Ann: Suzanne Seder
Supervisor
Tampa Convention Center
401 Channelside Drive
Tampa, FL 33602

Dear Ms. Seder:

Please accept this resume for a potential full-time job within the scope of event planning and Public Relations. Your company seems to do exactly the type of work that I am attracted to. I am interested in learning about any job opportunities that the Tampa Convention Center has to offer. My job and leadership experience, my major in Communication at Michigan State University, and my academic specialization in Public Relations qualify me for this type of work.

As you can see from the enclosed resume, I have had various leadership experiences including Greek Week Steering Committee and Senior Class Council I have taken several classes that focus on Public Relations and journalistic writing styles. I also had a year-long internship within the public relations field. I am now interested in seeking a frill-time job that will add depth and additional experience to my academic studies. My intense work ethic, enthusiastic attitude, strong self-motivation, and oral and written communication skills will prove valuable in contributing to the Tampa Convention Center's strategies.

I hope you will consider my request for a personal interview to discuss further my qualifications. I can be reached at (813) *xxx-xxxx* or by e-mail at amanda@aol.com. Thank you for your time and I hope to hear from you in the future.

Sincerely,
Amanda Graul

Apart from the fact that Amanda is a decent writer, nothing in this letter would catch the interest of a decision maker and Amanda did not receive a phone call.

I met her via a referral of a client and began to teach her the targeted search strategy right away. My direction to Amanda was that she identify topical issues that were current and relevant to the Ice Palace as an organization.

KEY NOTE: Exactly what you are looking for during your research is **inexact**; the topics are only discovered during the research and rarely, if ever, pre-determined, you just need a nose for topical, interesting, trendy issues.

For the Ice Palace, the main issue Amanda discovered in a Google search turned out to be their status as a potential host for the 2004 Republican National Convention (at the time, it was Fall 2002).

The article Amanda found on the Internet was as follows:

TAMPA PREENS TO SWAY GOP'S SELECTION PANEL
Up against New York and New Orleans, Tampa must prove it can handle the convention. By D. KARP, © St. Petersburg Times, published August 6, 2002

TAMPA -- The wining and dining begins tonight.
The area's Republicans spent Monday finalizing elaborate plans to woo the delegation that will decide what city will host the 2004 Republican National Convention.
And, like any hopeful suitor, the local host committee wants to look its best. Workers trimmed palm trees by the Tampa Convention Center and planted flowers on Ashley Drive, the main thoroughfare into downtown Tampa.
They put up signs at Tampa International Airport and rehearsed the minute-by-minute plan for the three-day visit by the GOP site selection committee.
"First impressions are critical when you are trying to win something," said Al Austin, co-chairman of the local host committee. "We will bend over backward to do everything to please them."
Tampa is competing against New Orleans and New York, two cities with reputations for putting on national political conventions. The nine-member site selection group will recommend a winner this fall, probably after the elections. The convention is scheduled for Aug. 31 to Sept. 4, 2004.
To compete, Tampa must show that its hotels, convention center and downtown arena can accommodate thousands of delegates and out-of-town journalists, Austin said.
"Once we do that, it puts us on a level playing field," Austin said.
One of the biggest challenges will be selling the area's landscape of hotels, which are spread out over two counties... Since learning 2 1/2 weeks ago that the Republican National Convention Site Selection Committee would visit Tampa, organizers have been planning every minute of the visit.

"We are pretty much working 24-7 at this point," said Karen Brand, the marketing vice president at the Tampa Bay Convention & Visitors Bureau. ... The delegates will compare logistics while in Tampa and New York. At about 3:30 p.m., the GOP committee will touch down at TIA, where preschoolers and pirates from Ye Mystic Krewe of Gasparilla will greet them with roses. Then they'll take a bus to International Plaza. ... Margie Kincaid, chairwoman of the Hillsborough County Republican Party, said organizers would do whatever it takes to impress. Even "our sunshine is better down here than anywhere else," she said. "With all the nice gulf breezes, it is going to be glorious. They will think they have died and gone to heaven."

She then went directly to the main source, the Ice Palace home web site, www.icepalace.com and started reviewing recent press releases. This led her to uncover a news release quoting the VP of Public Relations who announced that the Ice Palace had been selected as one of four potential sites (ironically, they weren't the site that was eventually picked, that honor belongs to New York City). This bit of sleuthing, led Amanda to rewrite her cover letter with information reflecting her research that she then sent to the Director of Season Sales, two weeks after the first cover letter she had sent, with the cover letter reading as follows:

AMANDA GRAUL AFTER   *BULLS-EYE COVER LETTER*

Chad Johnson
Director of Season Sales
Ice Palace
401 Channelside Dr., Tampa, FL 33602

Dear Mr. Johnson:

Congratulations on being chosen as one of the potential venues to host the 2004 Republican National Convention! It must be a very exciting time for you and your company.

I know I could be beneficial to many departments in your organization, although my education and key interests lie in event planning and public relations. As you can see from the enclosed resume, I have had various leadership experiences including Greek Week Steering Committee and Senior Class Council. I always jump at the opportunity to take on a challenge.

I have held several jobs that allowed me to work directly with the public while serving and fulfilling the needs of guests and clients. A year-long internship within the public relations field afforded me invaluable experience and a great deal of knowledge, tam now interested in seeking a full-time job that will allow me to grow along with the company, both personally and professionally. My intense work ethic, enthusiastic attitude, strong self-motivation, and oral and written communication skills will prove valuable in contributing to the Ice Palace's strategies.

I'm not sure if or where you may need a new associate but I can assure you that I would make an outstanding team member. I hope you will consider my request for a personal interview to discuss further my qualifications.

I can be reached at (813) xxx-xxxx or by e-mail at amanda@aol.com. Thank you for your time and I hope to hear from you in the future.

Sincerely,

Amanda Graul

The result. Amanda won an interview and was hired as the Ice Palace's Suite Services Coordinator.

Real Client Example 2: Celeste Jenkins – SALES PROFESSIONAL

Here is a professional that wanted to continue working for a Fortune 500 company, namely the second largest company in the world, General Electric. She had been downsized from another large corporate division and was scrambling to land a new job. Her research led to uncovering a very important issue to GE, namely that they were focusing on a little known federal regulation called HIPPA - HEALTH INSURANCE PORTABILITY & ACCOUNTABILITY ACT OF 1996.

Specifically, Celeste learned that HIPPA would drive a number of technology initiatives and new product launches by GE to help hospitals, healthcare providers and medical practitioners to protect the confidentiality of workers as they move from one job to another. Let's say you suffered from cancer and your job search landed you an interview at Frito Lays, it's conceivable that a Fritos Lay HR Manager could find out your ailment before you were hired and quite plausibly not hire you due to your health history. This type of discrimination could be done without the company ever being caught. HIPPA became a Federal Law enacted by Congress to protect the rights of worker's privacy of their health records.

Celeste's research uncovered, via the GE Home web page, a letter by Joe Hogan, the CEO of GE's health care division where he mentioned HIPPA four times.

-ARTICLE FOUND ON GE'S CORPORATE WEBSITE-

HEALTH INSURANCE PORTABILITY AND ACCOUNTABILITY ACT

Message from Joe Hogan
The next few years hold sweeping changes for the healthcare industry with the task of implementing Privacy and Security regulations such as the USA Health Insurance Portability and Accountability Act (HIPAA) regulations. These new regulations are an important step forward in protecting patient's privacy and improving efficiency within the healthcare industry. GE Healthcare is aware of the many patient care and business issues you may face as you implement actions to comply with Privacy regulations.
I am writing to assure you that GE is committed to conformance with all regulations and has always been committed to privacy and security. You can rely on GE to provide flexible clinical solutions to assist you in protecting the privacy and security

of your clinical workflow, as well as in safeguarding the confidentiality of your patient records.

To that end, we are continually assessing the security and privacy capabilities of all of our products and services. Please be assured that our products, software and services already contain many features that will help you comply with the privacy requirements. We are committed to working with you and to providing additional value to help you meet the continuing privacy challenge.

I want to thank you for your continued support of GE. We recognize the importance of providing you with healthcare tools that meet your patient's needs. We are dedicated to serving you now and in the future.

Sincerely,

[signature]

Joseph M. **Hogan**
President & **CEO**
GE Healthcare

This research led me to writing the following cover letter for Celeste:

Celeste's New Bulls-Eye Cover letter

Dear Mr. Hogan,

I read with interest your statements regarding GE's commitment to making products, software and services that meet HIPPA security and privacy standards. Since HIPPA is revolutionizing how electronic records are managed, transferred and protected, it is obvious that GE needs a team of sales executives who can stamp your Six Sigma Methodology on this initiative. Although my current BDM role at GE Information Technology Systems is being eliminated due to streamlining the division, I still want to put GE's investment in training me to good use by offering to contribute to pursue new HIPPA opportunities.

As a sales professional, I've handled account management duties where my results exceeded expectations on account development, winning market share, improving revenues and beating the competition. I've participated with numerous product launches/extensions where I dramatically improved sales, opened dozens of new accounts, solidified my customer base and brought stability to the territory.

I've truly enjoy being part of a business where I compete with the best and biggest in the industry and now look forward to another challenging sales opportunity that will allow me to apply client management, marketing and organizational skills. I want to align with an aggressive sales team that needs hands-on sales representative with a burning desire to win.

Sincerely,

Celeste Jenkins

Celeste's Result: What's noteworthy about this example is that Celeste started researching something she had never heard of before, in this case, national legislation to protect worker's healthcare records privacy. But that is the exact point of the research, your looking for something unique. Secondly, Celeste uncovers a Position Statement from the CEO – John Hogan (the top exec at GE's multi-billion dollar Health Care Division). Imagine a sales representative writing to the CEO of a huge international corporate division (to put this in perspective, GE Health Care is larger than half of the Fortune 500), and receiving a personal response from the CEO's office within a weak of writing the letter.

Real Client Example **3. JOHN ZILM - Human Resources**

John first finds a job that he is interested in, Regional HR manager for the Kelloggs Company. Now using the Targeted Search strategy, his goal is to connect with top executives at Kelloggs who he has never met. Although it was relatively easy to find a job opening, the difficult thing is getting your resume to a key decision maker who can pass it along from the top down. Therefore, by Googling Kelloggs, John came across this gem.

KELLOGG TAPS DAVIDSON TO HEAD U.S. SNACKS

BATTLE CREEK, Mich., May 21 /PRNewswire-FirstCall/

- Kellogg Company (NYSE: K) today announced that it has named Brad Davidson as its new president of the U.S. Snacks Division, effective June 9, 2003. That post has been vacant since February, and its responsibilities were handled by David Mackay, executive vice president and president, Kellogg USA. Davidson will report directly to Mackay.

A 19-year veteran of Kellogg, Davidson has spent the past three years as executive vice president, chief customer officer of Kellogg's U.S. Morning Foods Division. In that role, he led a major restructuring of Morning Foods' sales force, which contributed to dramatic improvements in business results, category share, customer relationships, and customer service. Previously, he had held numerous senior level sales and marketing positions, both in the U.S. and Canada.

"We conducted a thorough search, interviewing both internal and external candidates," said Carlos Gutierrez, Kellogg's chairman and chief executive officer. "Brad's leadership skills, proven record of accomplishments, and sales expertise make him best suited for this role."

Kellogg's U.S. Snacks Division has been undergoing a transformation from an acquire-and-integrate strategy to one of sustainable, organic growth. Mackay stepped in to directly oversee this strategic shift, which has involved a reorganization of the direct store door distribution (DSD) sales force to better align with our customer base, as well as a rationalization of stock- keeping units and a substantial increase in brand-building and innovation activity. He will spend the next couple of months transitioning Davidson into his new role.

Mackay said, "Brad will be able to step in and have an immediate impact. He is a proven leader with outstanding business instincts and execution skills. He will have an experienced team behind him, including Jim Holton, a 21-year Keebler veteran who runs our DSD sales force. I have full confidence that Brad will lead this business to dependable growth going forward."

Replacing Davidson as senior vice president, chief customer officer of U.S. Morning Foods will be George Ball. Ball has worked for Kellogg Company since 1976, and is currently senior vice president and general manager of Warehouse Club and Retail

Specialty Brands. Previously, he held several other leadership positions in Canada and the United Kingdom, and was managing director of Kellogg's Central American business.

Mark Wagner, currently vice president, customer teams, for U.S. Snacks, will be promoted to Ball's position. Wagner has worked in the Company's DSD sales force for the past 20 years, including six years as regional vice president of the Great Lakes region.
Gutierrez commented, "These moves reflect the depth of talent we have in our management team. These are very important roles in our Company, and each of these individuals has proven leadership skills and business expertise. These transitions will be seamless, and they also will allow David Mackay to devote more of his time to running Kellogg USA as a whole."

As you can read, the press release announced that Kelloggs had named a new divisional President, Brad Davidson, for the US Snacks Division (a $1.5 billion business unit). It also noted that George Ball (SVP of Retail Specialty Brands) would fill Davidson's old role and that Mark Wagner, VP of Customer Teams for US Snacks would fill George Ball's previous position. The final piece of the puzzle that came out of the press release was this statement: "Kellogg's US Snacks Division has been undergoing a transformation from an acquire-and-integrate strategy to one of sustainable, organic growth," now this may appear to some readers as somewhat elusive as to what this means, so let me try to clarify for you. The Fortune 500 are all publicly held and are expected to grow quarterly profits, year after year. In order to meet this lofty expectation, they typically take one of the following actions, acquire smaller companies, merge with peers or launch new products. Due to the fickle nature of the consumer market, it is usually easier for corporations to grow through acquisitions rather than new product launches (i.e. organically).

So why is this important to share? John had just worked for a company that had spent the last five years buying their competitors and had tripled in size. His overview noted that he possessed heavy expertise with the integration of business acquisitions. John was a great candidate for the job opening of Snacks Foods Regional HR Manager role, that is, if he could get a top decision maker to evaluate his credentials.

JOHN'S NEW BULLS-EYE COVER LETTER

JOHN ZILM ——— 21941 S. BURR RIDGE DRIVE, JOLIET, IL 60431, PH. (815) 744-2832

August 5, 2003

Brad Davidson
President - U.S. Snacks Food Division
Kellogg Company

Detroit, MI

Dear Mr. Davidson:

While applying for the Snacks Foods Regional HR Manager role, I noted in a news release your appointment to President with the mandate to rollout Kellogg's "transformation from an acquire-and- integrate strategy to one of sustainable growth."

The reason why the release caught my attention is that you are dealing with the same problems I helped solve with the Chas. Levy Company, the third largest DSD supplier of magazines in the US. Their need, which is similar to Kellogs, was to achieve positive synergies from corporate acquisitions. Levy's situation was that it suffered competitive and fiscal disadvantages. They needed to integrate their multiple business acquisitions by resolving problems associated with duplicated logistics and redundancy in support staff to grow the organization intelligently.

My resume will explain the contributions I made to right size Levy and help it thrive during its most turbulent period in the past 100± year corporate history.

I would like to meet with you as a first step in joining your team so we could determine how I might be an asset to Kellogg's continued success.

Sincerely,

John Zilm

> **The result**: He was called by the VP of HR and flown to Battle Creek MI to interview for the Regional HR opening. He noted that the VP had been personally routed John's resume, by the chief administrative secretary, which lent credibility to his application.

Real Client Example 4. Joe Menard – I.T. Professional

Joe was a victim of the dot.com meltdown that occurred around 2001. Finding work had become an endless process of registering with online job boards, sending his resume to faceless and nameless corporations along with millions of other technology industry professionals and largely being ignored for all of his efforts. Joe had become so desperate that he had opened a small "technology consulting" business. This essentially meant that he would do computer work for friends and neighbors. By the time we met, he had been searching for a job for the better part of two years. What I learned was that Joe wanted to relocate from Chicago to his home state of Pennsylvania and find a job where the future company would pay for his relocation as well as offer compensation close to what he had earned previously as an IT Network Director.

After rewriting his resume, I taught him how to conduct targeted research, which led him to uncover the following article.

HOSPITALS INVEST IN INFORMATION TECHNOLOGY TO ADDRESS THE RISING COST OF HEALTH CARE

PITTSBURGH BUSINESS TIMES - AUGUST 1, 2003 BY MARIA GUZZO

The University of Pittsburgh Medical Center has been among the nation's 100 Most Wired hospitals for five years in a row. That the health system achieves that rank is no surprise considering its board has implemented a five-year plan to spend $500 million on information technology initiatives, doubling the normal annual expense.

But while the large UPMC health system may be spending more money than others, its reasons for doing so are the same as others. Hospital officials report that they're using IT software and hardware in attempts to lower the rising cost of health care delivery, improve patient care and meet federal regulations, such as complying with the Health Insurance Portability and Accountability Act of 1996.

PAYING FOR PROGRESS

While the UPMC board instilled this $500 million/five-year goal, the system's spending is still about average. UPMC averages 3.8 percent total IT spending in relation to its overall hospital budget.

Butler Hospital's average annual IT investment is $2.5 to $3 million, or 2 percent of the hospital's overall budget, said Butler Memorial Hospital's vice president of outpatient services Ken DeFurio.

West Penn-Allegheny Health System's senior director of information systems Christina Middlemiss said unlike other industries, health care typically spends less than 3 percent on IT, a statistic she said she gleaned from Stamford, Conn.-based Gartner Inc., a technology industry research organization.

"WPAHS is no exception to this industry norm," she said.

IT spending is still a small -- but growing -- part of hospitals' overall budgets. According to statistics from PricewaterhouseCoopers, hospitals spend 38 percent of their budget on labor costs, 18 percent on supplies and services, and 5 percent on technology. A July 2002 article in the business magazine Healthcare Informatics said a survey by Gartner found hospitals spent 3 percent of their budgets on IT in 1999, 3.08 percent in 2000 and 3.15 percent in 2001. In a 2001 study, the publication reported, Stamford, Conn.-based research and consulting firm META Group determined the banking and financial industries spent 6.09 percent of revenue on IT in 2000 and 6.50 percent in 2001, compared with about 4.81 percent in 2000 and 4.2 percent in 2001 for health care.

According to IDC and CompTIA forecasts, health care IT spending is expected to increase. Spending is expected to rise from $15.8 billion in 2003 to $18.2 billion in 2006, according to information from those research groups published in HealthLeaders magazine, a Nashville, Tenn.-based trade publication.

UPMC's most-wired ranking stemmed from a study by Hospitals & Health Networks, which is the journal of the American Hospital Association. The study found that among the ways hospitals used IT were: installing systems that create computerized physician order entry, produce picture archiving and communication, manage medication distribution and computerize patient records.

Local hospitals are doing the same.

Mr. DeFurio said BMU is installing a system to archive and retrieve medical images. Hospitals are taking X-ray and MRI images and moving them around their facilities in digital form, the same way families now often use digital instead of traditional film cameras to take pictures so they can send them across the Internet to relatives.

"This makes them the instantly available to the physicians and they can begin to make care decisions," he said.

At UPMC, its electronic health record initiative represents 65 percent of the $500 million investment, UPMC CIO Dan Drawbaugh said. As patients move through the UPMC system -- from their primary care physician, to specialists, to X-ray and labs -- their results follow them.

West Penn-Allegheny has finished development of a physician portal, which allows participating doctors to access patient data from anywhere -- office, home or vacation. The health system's in-house IT department used commercially available software to implement it, which is going live this month.

TRACKING OUTCOMES

Hospitals report it's money well spent.

Mr. Drawbaugh said that by installing software at UPMC that tracks medication orders from physicians to the pharmacy to the nurse to the patient, they've reduced the number of errors.

"We're seeing tremendous outcomes," Mr. Drawbaugh said. "We anticipated seeing outcomes, but these exceeded our expectations."

Mr. DeFurio said checks and balances are built into the software programs that BMH has installed over the past few years.

"We've automated medication distribution, so from the time the physician writes the order, the pharmacy issues it, the nurse delivers it to patients we know it's the right patient, dose, medication and time," Mr. DeFurio said. "We've seen a dramatic reduction in errors."

Within a year of using the technology, medication errors that result in patients being harmed or having to stay in the hospital longer were reduced by 39 percent, he said.

From this article, I gleaned the name of the CIO (Chief Information Officer) of UPMC, Dan Drawbaugh and that the hospital was one of the most technologically advanced institutions within the medical community. It wasn't hard to craft an opening sentence that reflected this research as the following cover letter illustrates.

Joe's New Bulls-Eye Cover letter

JOE MENARD
1532 Branford Lane, Naperville, IL 60564 • 630-904-5688

September 4, 2003

Dan Drawburgh
Chief Information Officer
University of Pittsburgh Medical Center
200 Lothrop St.
Pittsburgh, PA 15213-2582

Dear Mr. Drawburgh:

Congratulations on your fifth consecutive year in the Top 100 Most Wired Hospitals and Health Systems in the United States!

I found your comments describing how the health record initiative outcomes exceeded your expectations, as written in the Pittsburgh Business Times article, very interesting. The focus on HIPPA compliance and cost containment through IT software and hardware is also impressive; HIPPA is an area that I am pursuing as a career move.

The reason for my letter is that I've enjoyed successfully reducing cost from the IT infrastructure through design rationalization and supplier management. As such, there appears a possible fit where my contributions could help UPMC continue to succeed.

If you are interested in continuing to improve efficiency and operational effectiveness of the UPMC networking infrastructure, I would like to discuss how I might help. Attached is my resume for your review. I will contact you by phone to schedule a time when we can discuss this at length.

Sincerely,

Joe Menard

The result. Joe landed the job in 2003 and held it until early 2006.

Real Client Example **5 – Brad Bedoe**

Brad was a recent college graduate who wanted to parlay his love of bicycling into a fulltime job working at a bicycle manufacturer, preferably in the Chicago metro region. What he learned through a little research was that the largest bike manufacturer in Chicago was a company by the name of SRAM, which was the original creator of grip-shift technology. SRAM makes bicycle components including shifters, derailleurs, brakes, chains, and other bike parts.

With a little research he discovered the following press release.

SRAM CORPORATION AND ROCKSHOX TODAY ANNOUNCED THE COMPLETION OF SRAM'S ACQUISITION OF ROCKSHOX
ROCKSHOX, Inc. (RSHX.OB) - a leading developer of high performance mountain bike suspension products - today announced that it has completed the sale of the business to SRAM Corporation, which was earlier announced on February 19, 2002.

"We are very pleased to complete the sale process, and we are now completely focused on running the business and on integrating RockShox with SRAM," commented Bryan Kelln, President & CEO of RockShox. "Under SRAM's leadership, we are forming global integration teams, which will work together over the coming two months to put together specific objectives, plans and timelines. Later this spring, we will have a specific set of initiatives designed to integrate the businesses, enhance customer satisfaction, and accelerate product development, all the while reducing the cost structure."

"We look forward to building on what the RockShox team has achieved over the past few years. They drove significant restructuring, taking out more than $10 million in cost. In addition, they truly enhanced the product line and gained market share. They have created a nice platform from which we can continue to improve," commented Stan Day, President of SRAM corporation. "Now, with our combined product development capabilities, RockShox' strength in the mountain bike segment and SRAM's strength in the pavement sector, we are poised to take both businesses to a higher level of performance. Clearly the strategic fit made sense for the industry; with our complementary product lines we can bring more value to the global bicycle business in a "one stop shopping" environment. We see a clear path to enhanced and integrated product lines, a better cost structure, and superior customer service. Our objective in the integration will be to merge the strengths each company brings to the table. Each business can help the other move to the next level."

This article led me to write the following letter to the President of Sram.

Brad's New Bulls-Eye Cover letter

Stan Day
President & Chief Executive Officer
SRAM Corporation
1333 North Kingsbury, 4th Floor
Chicago, IL 60622

Dear Mr. Day, congratulations on acquiring RockShox!

I enjoyed reading Bike Magazine's coverage on how SRAM is poised to remain an industry leader. What caught my attention is the fierce battle you are in with Shimano. I think that there are plenty of opportunities to help SRAM beat Shimano in every category in which you compete, and if possible, I want to enlist as a SRAM *soldier* and promote your products in the marketplace. If you allow me to say so, I've been a fan for some time. In high school, as a mechanic at Crystal Lakes Ski & Bike Shop, I saw my first SRAM Grip Shift and discovered the beauty of your efficient designs. Obviously, I'm preaching to the choir, but I want to demonstrate sincere appreciation for your visionary innovations.

What excites me is your pioneering approach to pushing the limits of innovation in the areas of product development, branding and business marketing. Could I fit into SRAM's future? I'm not sure if or where you may need a new associate, but I can bring value immediately in a selling capacity, a marketing role or a combination of the two.

I've published stories that directly contributed to increased exposure and funds for organizations and their causes. In addition, working at Towers Productions, Inc. (a Chicago based content provider for A&E, Discovery and History Channels) allowed me to contribute creatively on their cable tv programming team. I can use my passion for biking to support win additional publicity for your efforts to make bicycles part of the Senate's Energy Bill. This is just one of many ideas, please call me to let me know when we could talk in detail.

Sincerely,

Brad Bedoe

SUMMARY OF A TARGETED CAREER SEARCH

Incorporate traditional research to justifiably speak with decision makers at a target company. In other words, use research to open the door and meet with decision makers at targeted companies, this allows you to create a career network from scratch.

Snapshot   ***Bulls-eye Search Letters*** are written with information you uncovered from industry specific research of corporate press releases, Google searches or by using your local library's databases for company specific articles. Once you research the target company, you can leverage this data into content for the cover letter and make initial contact with decision makers.

This approach is useful for any industry and can be done with zero financial cost. If we use the analogy of a dart board, you will be gathering data on a few companies that represent the bulls-eye. In general, you need to research between 10-30 companies to land a position.

I have used these techniques to turn a hotel floor manager into a Wall Street Banker. A secretary at an Eye Doctors' office into a sales executive, and a lawn-mower salesman into a corporate trainer in a Big 6 accounting firm.

ACTION STEP SUMMARY
1. Go to main library.
   - Find the Reference Librarian - Business Section - ask him or her how to use their online article databases such as OCLC, ABI/Inform, InfoTrac and FirstSearch.

2. Target 15-30 companies that interest you
   - Review a corporation's marketing literature, press releases and annual reports to uncover current events spanning an 18-month timeframe (the past 12 months and the prospective 6 months). Look for new directions that a company is taking (two examples that I found in the past that are a little dated now were Coke sponsoring the Atlantic Olympics, 3Com buying US Robotics).

3. Write targeted cover letters to the people who are quoted in the articles you read.
   - Make sure you cover letter references your research. Repeat again and again until hire.

CHAPTER 2
COVER LETTERS FOR JOB ADVERTISEMENTS

I AM regularly asked, "Do you need a cover letter with a resume?" "Yes" is the simple answer. Although cover letters are not as important as the resume itself, they are critical to winning job offers. I tell clients that cover letters are like ties, although smaller and less expensive than a suit, they are an essential complement to the suit, and the finishing touch that makes the outfit look great – assuming you pick the right combination.

Cover letters are brief narratives that are approximately three paragraphs long with each paragraph, more or less, addressing the following:

- Paragraph 1) introduces your interest in the company, the job you are seeking or the job opening that you saw posted or in the newspaper.
- Paragraph 2) briefly explains why you are a good fit for the role.
- Paragraph 3) simply closes the letter politely by asking for the opportunity to interview.

At the beginning, if possible, cover letters should be personalized to the attention of a real person. With that said, it is not always feasible that you will know who the person is that you need to make the letter to the attention of, in that case, you can use the standard general opening; To whom it may concern, or Dear Hiring Manager or dear Human Resource Manager.

The first paragraph can simply state your interest in working for ____ (fill in the blank) company. It is perfectly acceptable to be a little excessively enthusiastic here and tell your audience that you have always wanted to be a: waiter, sales clerk, administrative assistant, even if this is just a part time job that is helping you earn Summer money. In other words, tell your audience what they want to hear and they want to know that you are excited to work for their company.

The second paragraph is where you need to get personal. If you are tying to get a job as an office worker, try to identify any correlative experience you might have at school, helping your parents or previous work that could touch on why you will be a great asset to the prospective company.

The final paragraph is a simple closure of the letter and takes one or two sentences. Thank you for reviewing my resume and I look forward to the possibility of an interview at your convenience.

Steve Tersh Job Advertisement.

Job Title	**Vision Care Territory Manager**
Req #	1933BR
Job Description	This Territory Manager will cover the Memphis, and Little Rock, TN area. Executing Sales calls on eye doctors (Optometrists, Ophthalmologists) and other optical locations to promote our contact lenses and contact lens solutions in a consultative selling approach. This would involve the private/independent doctor as well as retail optical locations. Develop and maintain an effective routing and zoning plan for the territory. Develop and implement account specific programs and business plans. Actively participate in National and Regional Sales meetings. Implement and follow all administrative policies and programs. Assess/Analyze doctor's business needs to gain positioning of Bausch & Lomb products. Maintain routine call cycle of 30 calls per week. Successful certification from completion of home study, classroom training, preceptorships and co-travels and examinations within the first 6 months of employment. Seeking opportunities for strategic business planning (expansion of B&L product utilization in an account) and portfolio selling.
Qualifications	BA/BS required. 3-5 years business to business sales experience. Must have documented superior sales success. Must be able to demonstrate a thorough understanding of the sales process. Proven ability to self manage time and administrative tasks (pre-post call planning, territory routing/zoning, expenses, sample accountability, etc.) Computer skills (microsoft applications and intranet navigation), Interpersonal skills, strong written and verbal communication skills.
Work Location	TN - Memphis
Full Time/Part Time/Internship	Full-Time
Career Area	Sales & Marketing

B. STEVE TERSH

438 N. Harvey, Oak Park, IL 60302, 708-445-9020 • tersh438@yahoo.com

May 11, 2004

Bausch & Lomb
Req. # 1377BR

     I am forwarding this letter and my resume in response to your opening for a Vision Care Territory Manager. The reason the opportunity caught my attention is how the job description so neatly fits my professional profile. As you can read, my selling experience spans a wide set of responsibilities which includes account prospecting, account management and business development within a highly competitive environment.

     Professionally, my objective is to continue a demanding account executive sales career in a position that will best capitalize on my technical, consulting and strategic selling abilities. Although I am a seasoned performer in the business arena, it is also worth noting that I possess compelling academic qualifications. In order to stay aware of emerging business trends and opportunities, I recently completed an MBA in Management, at the Lake Forest Graduate School of Management.

     At Pitney Bowes much of my work is complexly technical in nature which requires that I constantly monitor changes in market dynamics, stay abreast of competitive pressures and analyze client driven demands. The combination of having worked in account sales, along with an advanced degree in business management demonstrates a multi-tasking personality that will help me become an immediate asset to your sales team.

     In my position, I maintain a busy schedule providing client service support, directing sales development efforts and executing our corporate business plans. I have learned to remain flexible while allocating resources efficiently to maximize sales potential.

     Overall, you will find that I am innovative, resourceful and capable of handling all levels of project development responsibilities, in other words, I desire to remain a key contributing factor of a company's marketing and sales success. Thank you for taking the time to review my background.

Sincerely,

B. Steve Tersh
Salary History   1997 $40,000   Present $65,000 + bonus

Takeda Pharmaceuticals Career Section

Sales Representative - Aurora, IL (P) – 0500385

Job Description

(Apply Online)

Description

Uniquely Takeda...It's a commitment to helping people worldwide.
At Takeda, we're building our company the right way by putting people first. It's a commitment to the patients we serve and to the employees who share our passion for making a difference. We're working together to improve life worldwide. And we're inviting you to join us.

You will perform the following functions in this key role:

Promotes and sells Takeda products.
Contacts physicians by phone and in person to promote Takeda products.
Distributes product samples and marketing literature to physicians and other healthcare professionals.
Generates sales contact opportunities by calling private physician offices and healthcare organizations.
Follows-up with physicians to gather feedback and questions on experience with Takeda products.
Provides approved information to physicians on Takeda products, e.g. proper medical usage, dosage amounts and side effects.
Ensures that physicians are adequately stocked with Takeda products and distributes ordering information.
Provides feedback to sales management on customer requests, responses to promotions and product access.

Qualifications
You must possess the following requirements and experience to succeed in this position:
Bachelor's Degree.

Preferred:
Experience in Pharmaceutical sales.

Skills:
Communications: ability to communicate ideas and data both verbally and written.
Relationship building: ability to make and maintain client and prospect contact with physicians.
Organization: ability to maintain accurate and detailed records of appointments, sales, calls, follow-up calls, samples.
Time Management: ability to set priorities and workflow to accomplish day-to-day tasks in a timely manner

Profile

Job Field	Field Sales
Locations	US-IL-Aurora
Schedule	Full-time
Job Level	Individual Contributor
Education Level	Bachelor's Degree (±16 years)

31

ANNE COLE

1615 N. Cleveland Ave., 1S, Chicago, IL 60614
H: 312-573-0735 • C: 312-286-7110

Takeda Pharmaceuticals
Re: Sales Representative – Aurora, IL – 0500385

I am pursing the direct sales position posted on your career section. As you can see from the attached resume, my selling experience demonstrates a fit as described in the opening since you want professionals who can execute business development plans that deliver customers and revenues. As for my personality, I have an achievement-focused mentality that is based on attainting specific goals quickly and consistently exceeding expectations. I've won sales awards and received management commendation for bringing creative strategies to bear in my account development efforts. Whether I am challenged with negotiating large contracts for services or launching new products into the marketplace I make it a personal goal to overachieve. I can say that a key capability is matching customer needs to products, services, programs and solutions.

My work history integrates strategic tactics that include aggressive account prospecting, high-level presentations, territory management as well as collaborating with internal teams that were created for the sole purpose of rolling out enterprise-wide projects.

Over the past 7 years I have participated in numerous product launches/extensions and executed selling programs targeting small, medium and Fortune 500 sized businesses. I am resourceful at attaining dramatic sales growth, opening new accounts, solidifying the customer base and bringing stability to my assigned territory.

I've truly enjoyed being part of businesses where I compete with the best and biggest in the industry. I am now looking forward to another challenging sales opportunity that will allow me to apply client development, marketing and organizational skills. I want to align with an aggressive company that seeks a hands-on sales representative who has a burning desire to win. Given the opportunity, you will find me capable of handling increased responsibilities, able to communicate effectively and experienced at resolving complex problems.

I look forward to the opportunity to discuss in further detail your needs and my specific qualifications for this position.

Sincerely,

Anne Cole

W. R. BERKLEY CORPORATION

◄ Back to search results

Apply for this job   **Email to a friend**

Title:	**IT Manager**
Skills:	Strong technical management skills, insurance industry background, excellent communication skills, SQL Server, Hperion Essbase and Visual Basic preferred
Date:	7-19-2004
Location:	Chicago, IL
Area code:	**630**
Tax term:	**FULLTIME**
Pay rate:	DOE
Length:	
Position ID:	023589
Dice ID:	10112867

Job description:

** Please forward your salary requirements along with your resume.

Responsible for IT for a small but rapidly growing commercial property and casualty insurance company. The primary responsibilities of this position are:

* Development and implementation of executive, financial and customer information systems, including Data **Warehouse**
* Coordinating and developing automated processes for transfer of data to/from unaffiliated third parties
* Training end-users on all internally developed systems
* Effectively leading a team and working hands on with the team
* Interface effectively with all business units to understand the business strategy and provide the proper information solutions to meet company objectives

The position initially reports to the Chief Financial Officer but is expected to report directly to the President within two years.

Experience

Must have 2 to 4 years of Project Leader experience, at least 1 year of multiple project management experience.

Must have insurance industry experience.

Must have data **warehousing** experience.

Skills

Must be able to quickly identify with the corporate mission and identify how IT

Brett's targeted job advertisement, page 2.

compliments the organizational goals.

Must be able to communicate effectively with senior management.

Strong technical management skills, sound decision-making skills, conflict resolution skills, outstanding communication skills.

Must have a demonstrated ability to set and manage to aggressive project time lines

Must have a basic understanding of software development methodologies and the ability to work with simultaneous projects that have constant aggressive deadlines.

SQL Server, Hyperion Essbase and Visual Basic skills preferable.

Education

MIS or IT college degree required.

Travel required: none
Telecommute: no

Apply for this job   Email to a friend

To place this job in your Saved Jobs folder, log in **or click** here **to register.**

Contact for more information:
Nancy Micale
Berkley Technology Services
475 Steamboat Rd

Greenwich, CT 06830

Phone: (203) 629-3087
Fax: (203) 629-3073
E-mail: nmicale@wrberkley.com
Web: http://www.wrberkley.com

Dice
Tech Jobs. Tech Talent.

W. R. BERKLEY
CORPORATION

Back to search results

Feedback | Help | Jobs at Dice | Security Tips | Privacy Statement | Terms & Conditions

BRETT W. QUERHAMMER

533 Chicago Ave. #C, Evanston, IL 60202 • 847.736.7193
bquerhammer@comcast.net

Nancy Micale
Position ID: 023589
IT Manager
W.R. Berkley Corporation

Dear Ms. Micale:

I am responding to your company posting for a Manager of IT with Insurance and Data Warehousing experience. As my background indicates, I have subject matter expertise that applies to a broad range of business fields and have rolled out leading-edge data management technologies and technical architectures involving multidimensional analysis, measurement and comparison of corporate data assets.

As a professional, my work history spans two companies and five progressive functional titles. Originally at Accenture and presently with Focal Communications, I've lead projects that deal specifically with the aggregation, manipulation, storage and retrieval of business intelligence or financial information. It is worth noting that all three of the key projects outlined at Focal Communications were data-centric and the two key clients I supported at Accenture were Aon and Allstate.

As an IT Manager, the numerous projects I've contributed to launching touch on reorganizing, automating and streamlining business systems or operations at both regional and national levels. This experience sharpened the team leadership, executive communication and problem solving abilities that a manager needs to possess and will help me adapt quickly in your corporate culture.

The summation of my professional experience is a successful track record of developing and implementing strategic plans that affect daily systems operations for the entire corporation. My desire is to align with an company that seeks a manager with vision, seasoning and integrity. I believe it would be mutually rewarding for us to set up an interview. Once I learn more about your specific needs, I can outline how I will add value and contribute to your team.

Sincerely,

Brett W. Querhammer

3. STRATEGIC PLANNING MANAGER

Company: BJC HealthCare Location: St. Louis, MO 63110
Status: Full Time, Employee Job Category: Healthcare - Other
Relevant Work Experience: 2+ to 5 Years Career Level: Experienced (Non-Manager)
Education Level: Master's Degree

Monster recommends using Apply Now. Learn more.

Job Description

BJC HealthCare is one of the largest nonprofit healthcare organizations in the United States, delivering services to residents primarily in the greater St. Louis, southern Illinois and mid-Missouri regions. Our nationally recognized hospitals and affiliation with Washington University School of Medicine ensures our goal to improve the health of the people and communities we serve.

BJC currently has the opportunity for an experienced Strategic Planning Manager.

Position Purposes: This position has responsibility for leading major planning projects for hospital presidents, to include strategic planning, clinical service lines planning, and performing significant financial, analytical, and strategic analysis.

Principal Accountabilities and Essential Duties of the Job:

Manage client (SEOs, presidents, entity directors and BJC business managers) relationships and planning expectations
- Surface business opportunities that advance business priorities
- Develop sound analysis and proposals based on data
- Draw conclusions based on analysis and advance recommendations
- Present results to decision-makers (Boards, senior executives, medical staff) as needed
- Follow-up on open issues to gain resolution
- Transition plans to implementation stage and follow-up on results
- Manage internal and-or client resources in completing project work

Manage project resources effectively
- Use state-of-the-art planning (analytical tools and research)
- Set and modify project priorities to address client expectations and hospital priorities
- Independently plan and organize work flow for projects
- Manage internal and/or client resources in completing project work
- Conducts work in an organized, efficient manner.
- Ensures on-time completion of high-quality deliverables.

Develop network (external and internal) for maintaining current market and BJC intelligence
- Surface synergies and conflicts regarding BJC initiatives
- Provide consultation to business mangers regarding planning approaches
- Use resources to build competitive intelligence

- Facilitate complex discussions at a senior management level (i.e., hospital executive teams, medical staff) in a manner which builds consensus across parties

Special Duties:

- Work on priority projects as assigned by the Senior Leadership Group. Work with other business units in the development of their business plans.
- Develop and maintain a market, industry, and competitive intelligence information system to serve BJC business units and System senior management.
- Oversee development of the competitive analysis reports, and identify opportunities and risks for BJC business units created by competitor positioning.

Develop and give oral and written presentations at a senior executive level, demonstrating the ability to influence senior leadership decision making through:

- Developing close partnership with individual leaders
- Clearly expressing key messages
- Facilitating difficult conversations on complicated strategic issues
- Gaining credibility for self, department and BJC HealthCare through demonstrating strong intellectual rigor and an ability to respond credibly to pointed and difficult questions.

IGOR ZHIZHIN ——————— **3114 Riverside Dr., Sunnyvale, CA 92374**

BJC HealthCare
Re. Strategic Planning Manager

Dear recruiter,

The role of Strategic Planning Manager (5PM) caught my attention after carefully reading the expectations and purpose of the position. If I understand correctly, a critical element of the SPM succeeding at BJC HealthCare is the project orientation of the duties and direct interaction with senior executives of various hospitals. As you can see from my resume, three of my past four roles involved planning and execution of strategic projects that impacted revenues, market share and efficient business building tactics. It is important to note the collaboration between myself CEO, Board of Directors and VPs of my company as well as our client senior managers related to services and product offerings for the healthcare industry.

My viability to fill the opening is also indicated by a successful history as a market-builder, account developer and client manager in globally competitive business environments. Professionally, my BDM role at New York City Ambulette, albeit brief, was an intense focus on navigating the business landscape to move this 15 year-old business into position to rapidly increase revenues and expand business presence in traditional and non-traditional markets. At American Express, I hit the ground running, and within two months, ranked in the top percentile of performers as relating to customer acquisition and development. The American College of and Monem positions allowed me to execute organizational and planning duties to help the enterprise accomplish wide-ranging business goals.

Currently, I am seeking another challenging opportunity that will demand my full potential. My desire is to align with a healthcare company that is competing for market share, sales and profitability. If you seek a professional who thrives under pressure, is a skilled multi-tasker and exceeds goals consistently, I am sure my profile will meet your expectations. The ideal opportunity will allow me to contribute at a company that is committed to rapid expansion or is repositioning itself to compete in new markets.

Given the opportunity, you will find me dedicated, innovative and resourceful with a focus on handling increasingly demanding expectations. I would appreciate the opportunity to discuss present or projected needs that you are experiencing. Thank you for taking the time to review my background.

Sincerely,

Igor Zhizhin

TINA BROWN

✉ 280 Nevins St., Brooklyn, NY 11217
☎ 773-871-8777 or 718-522-9470 ✉Email tbb62@hotmail.com

hr@marthastewart.com
Ref Code: Sr. Editor – Weddings
Martha Stewart Living Omnimedia
11 West 42nd Street
New York, NY 10036

Dear HR Manager,

I am forwarding my resume in response to your search for a Weddings Editor. As you can read, my experience as a Photo Art Director, Photo Shoot Assistant and Freelance commercial Artist is balanced with the underlying principals in art that I gained by completing a BFA at Chicago's reputable Art Institute. Although I feel that I am a creative/artistic professional, it is worth noting that in addition, I am a capable business manager with strengths in operational, organizational and planning duties that I have used to successfully complete numerous creative projects over the past 10 years.

Although I enjoy my position Photo Art Director at Ambrosi & Associates, the opportunity that is described in your posting appears an exciting one that will challenge me to continue maximizing my full professional potential. What motivates me to consider the move can be boiled down to the desire to align myself with a progressive company that is universally respected as a shaper of culture and consumer taste. If given the opportunity, you will see that I possess the vision and confidence to meet all expectations and will be able to bring value to your existing staff.

I would appreciate the opportunity to discuss the role during an interview at your convenience. Thank you for taking the time to review my background.

Sincerely,

Tina Brown

Chapter 3
Examples of
Personalized Cover Letters

March 31, 2001

Maunuvon Lueders
Vice President Sales
Oneworld

Dear Mr. Lueders,

Thank you for reviewing my credentials for the Regional Sales Manager Americas role that is currently open on the Oneworld team. I am excited to be presenting my qualifications due to what appears to be a great fit between the job description and my professional work history.

It is interesting that the position demands a leader who is willing to travel and demonstrates expertise with strategic planning, business development and client retention efforts in globally competitive business environments. As you can read from the attached resume, my current duties as a Regional Sales Manager for Finnair, and previously, as Regional Sales Representative for Malsysia Airlines, have developed the executive skills and creative expertise needed to generate revenue increases and successfully expand international sales territories. Since the role encompasses a number of operational elements, it is worth noting that I have a firm grounding in organizational and planning duties associated with leading staff to attain marketing, sales development and business plan execution goals.

I offer an in-depth background in working with Oneworld partners, having developed close working relationships with partner airlines in the Midwest region. I have successfully worked and lived in multi cultural settings, having lived in SE Asia for ten years and worked for both an Asian and European airline. This should communicate the ability to easily adapt to distinctly different cultures and indicate that I would be able to relocate and travel without restrictions. My experience at a progressive Oneworld member airline, leads me to welcome this new opportunity to contribute to the continued development and growth of the Oneworld alliance.

Given the opportunity, you will find me dedicated, innovative and resourceful with a focus on leading staff and preparing them to exceed expectations. I would appreciate the opportunity to discuss this opportunity at your convenience. Thank you for taking the time to review my background.

Sincerely,

Todd W. Arthur

December 11, 1995

Jonathan Van Oss
Director of Marketing Information System
AMERICAN MEDICAL ASSOCIATION
515 N. State, 15th Floor
Chicago, IL 60610

Dear Mr. Van Oss,

On the recommendation of Darlene Greathouse, I am forwarding this letter and resume regarding the List Director position that is currently open. After Darlene had explained her primary responsibilities at the AMA, we both came to the conclusion that this opportunity neatly fits my background in project development, market segmentation and strategic planning for new product introductions. As you can see from the project orientation of my work history, I have been involved with a broad spectrum of product/service marketing and direct sales activity. My interest in working for the AMA stems from the desire to find a career opportunity that allows me to continue providing marketing direction and project coordination, a position that will allow me to apply my full expertise and experience in vendor management, promotions, sales and negotiations.

During my professional career, I have handled progressively challenging management and operational responsibilities for both corporate and municipal organizations. My current position as an Assistant Buyer for Montgomery Ward's profitable Electric Avenue Home & Office division (consisting of over 250 stores) has taught me the necessary production skills and refined my creative capabilities which should allow me to become an immediate asset on your staff.

I would appreciate the opportunity to discuss my skills and potential contributions in further detail at your convenience. Thank you for taking the time to review my background.

Sincerely,

Debra Bell

CAROLYN CAPRANICA, C.P.M.
1168 S. Plymouth Court, 1SE, Chicago, IL 60605
Home: (312) 554-8581   Office: (312) 322-6667

March 14, 1994

Patricia Young
Commissioner
Metropolitan Water Reclamation District
 of Greater Chicago
100 East Erie St., Chicago, IL 60611

Dear Commissioner Young:

Please allow me to thank you in advance for taking the time to read the enclosed application for the position of Purchasing Agent.

I believe my experience in the Procurement/Materials Management profession for the past 13 years at the country's number one premier commuter railroad represents the experience you are looking for. Presently, I am the Director of Procurement responsible for purchasing material, supplies, equipment and services for all Metra departments with budget expenditures in excess of $85,000,000.

The procurement process at Metra is a fast-paced environment where deadlines are a priority and handling multiple jobs are the norm. My interpersonal skills have been strengthened by constant interaction and negotiations with Metra's executive staff, union employees and vendors. I'm organized, detail oriented and enjoy working with all levels management and personnel.

I am looking for a creative, challenging position and would like the opportunity to learn more about the Metropolitan Water Reclamation District. My experience and what you need sound like an ideal match. I look forward to hearing from you.

Sincerely,

Carolyn Capranica, C.P.M.

43

ELIZABETH A. EMMEL D.V.M

213 Washington Blvd., Apt. 2, Oak Park, IL, 60302 (708) 386-4729

Dr. Homas Kleven, D.V.M.
Emergency Veterinary Care South
13715 S. Cicero Ave.
Crestwood, Illinois 60445

Dear Dr. Kleven:

Please accept this letter and resume as application for the position of associate veterinarian at Emergency Veterinary Care South in Crestwood.

There are several skills in particular which I feel would make me an asset to your hospital:

- I have experience in veterinary emergency medicine obtained at one of the Chicagoland areas busiest emergency clinics.
- I placed a special emphasis on avian and exotic animal medicine and surgery while in veterinary school, taking all available elective courses and selecting externships which would give me an optimum amount of experience in this specialty.
- Prior to veterinary school I managed a 15 person research laboratory with a $750,000 annual budget. This experience made me familiar with working with precision under imposing time constraints, with many different types of people, within a rigid budget. I've since found all of these skills invaluable to me.

Should my qualifications meet the needs of your hospital, I would be delighted with the opportunity for a personal interview. If you need any additional information regarding my qualifications please do not hesitate to call.

Thank you for your time and consideration. I look forward to speaking with you in the near future.

Sincerely,

Elizabeth A. Emmel D.V.M.

W. GAIL FERGUSON
155 N. Harbor Dr., #130, Chicago, IL 60601 ① 312/565-0144

May 15, 1995

Sharon Wilko
Nurse Recruiter
RUSH-PRESBYTERIAN-ST. LUKE'S MEDICAL CENTER

Dear Ms. Wilko:

I am forwarding this letter, a current copy of my resume and the attendant transfer application forms in order to pursue the open position as a nursing career consultant (#131).

Since starting a career in the nursing profession, I have worked to improve the delivery of nursing care I provide to patients in coordination with the health care team. In addition to patient services, I have focused my professional capabilities on providing a level of service to my employers that is an example to my peers and an encouragement to my supervisors. My success in these efforts has encouraged me to seek opportunities in health care administration. I am now seeking a position that utilizes my professional skills in healthcare, an emphasis in quality team work, and an understanding of organizational support that is necessary to provide excellent consumer services.

I find working in the health care industry, challenging, mentally stimulating and it has encouraged me to meet my full potential. My professional history that involves clinical experience, continued education, and administrative skills will serve to help me become an immediate asset and to grow as a professional nurse. Hopefully you will see, from the enclosed resume, that I have demonstrated experience that will allow me to become an immediate asset to your staff.

I appreciate your consideration of my background and look forward to discussing, in detail, the responsibilities associated with possible positions.

Sincerely,

Gail Ferguson

FLORENCIO FERRAO
71 E. Wacker Dr. Chicago, IL 60601 312-346-7100

October 3, 1997

Meg Fisher
Vice President, Human Resources
FOUR SEASONS HOTELS AND RESORTS
900 N. Michigan, Ste., 840, Chicago, IL 60611

Dear Ms. Fisher,

First off, please allow me to congratulate you and the Four Seasons' team for the well deserved recognition in last month's Condé Nast Top 100 issue. It is impressive enough to note that the top two hotels are managed by Four Seasons, but a true testimony to consistent excellence is the fact that six other properties are also placed among the top 25 in North America. These rankings indicate the quality and expectation of your executive staff and reaffirms my desire to approach Four Seasons in order to consider present or future needs that my background might fit.

This letter and resume should give you some insight to the career direction that I am interested in pursuing. An ideal position is one that combines my experience in strategic planning, project execution, and property management oversight within the globally competitive business environment. Professionally, my management responsibilities within Taj International Hotels include my present position as General Manager of the Executive Plaza, and previously, as Food & Beverage Director at two other properties for this company. Overall this has developed the executive skills and creative expertise needed to generate revenue increases and successfully expand market share. Additionally, as a complement to administrative skills, I also have a firm grounding in the operational, organizational and planning duties associated with marketing and sales activities.

Although I truly enjoy my current position, I possess the vision and personal confidence to consider another challenging opportunity that will demand my full potential. My desire is to align myself with The Four Season's effort to win market position, implement cost management initiatives, customer service strategies and programs that build strong operational cohesion.

I would appreciate the opportunity to discuss present or projected needs that you are experiencing. Thank you for taking the time to review my background.

Sincerely,

Florencio Ferrao

ERI C H. FIELD

6417 N. Leavitt St., Chicago, 60645, (312) 973-5936

February 23, 1994

Mitchell D. Weiner
VP National Sales & Marketing
Archer Management Services
855 Avenue of the Americas
New York, NY 10001

Dear Mr. Weiner:

This letter and attached resume is being forwarded to your attention in response to your Chicago Tribune advertisement for a regional sales manager. Since beginning a sales career in 1980, I have concentrated on developing a substantial account base, negotiating profitable contracts and providing exemplary customer service and support to maintain client satisfaction. As a firm believer that hard work and innovation are keys to successful revenue results and the yard stick of a competent sales professional, I have worked diligently to sell over $3,700,000 of courier and facilities management services during the past 3 years.

Although I find my current position both mentally stimulating and personally rewarding, it does not demand my full potential. I am now looking for an assignment that will correlate my abilities to manage and develop accounts, generate substantial revenues and sell services to decision makers at the highest level. After reviewing my resume, I hope you will see that I can become an immediate asset to your organization.

I would appreciate the opportunity to discuss my skills and potential contributions to your company at your convenience.

Sincerely,

Eric Field

Salary History 1989-present: $36,000-$38,000

TONI FIELDS

4624 S. Maple, Berwyn, IL 60402 ☎cell 708/257-4480 ☎hm 708/788-3743

Dear Terri Williams:

I am writing to formally express my interest in the Cath Lab Manager position with Florida Hospital –Heartland Medical Center.

My initial exposure to management came from my involvement managing two family owned furniture businesses. Subsequently, in the health care arena, I gained supervisory experience when I was the Clinical Director in the Cardiac Cath Lab at Illinois Vascular Institute and Directed Lab Operations at the Bronchoscopy lab for Edward Hines V.A Hospital.

In the Cardiac Cath Lab I was responsible for all operations of a $3 million dollar, freestanding medical facility. I supervised and trained nursing and technical staff: I conducted orientations and on-the-job training in order to maintain the highest quality assurance, productivity and medical care standards. I supervised record maintenance and administered the budget. Additionally, I possess experience as a Cardiovascular Nursing Instruction in both classroom and laboratory environments at Medical Career Institute.

My diverse experience has developed me as a well-rounded professional. I am well aware of the value of teamwork and pride myself on my ability to foster a cooperative working environment. I excel in setting priorities and utilizing resources to ensure the highest standards of medical care. I am committed to the highest patient relations standards. I would like to apply my talents and skills to the position of Manager of the Cardiac Cath Lab ad Heartland Medical Center.

Thank you for your consideration; I look forward to talking to you further regarding this position.

Sincerely,

Toni Fields

TOM GUNDERSON

2234 W. Taylor #2R, Chicago IL 60612
Hm. 312.226.8741   Wk 312.559.6707

May 16, 1995

Mr. Ed Gannon
BLUE CROSS BLUE SHIELD OF FLORIDA, INC.
P.O. Box 44088
Jacksonville, FL 32231-4088

Dear Mr. Gannon:

On the recommendation of Mr. Robert Ard at CN&W, I am forwarding this letter and a current copy of my resume in order to pursue the Sr. Compensation Analyst position currently advertised in the Wall Street Journal for Blue Cross Blue Shield. I am very interested in a position that combines my compensation background that includes project development, facilitating program coordination and interdepartmental support services. For the past five years these experiences have allowed me to be involved with the entire spectrum of human resources.

As you can see from the resume, I have kept a busy itinerary handling progressively challenging management responsibilities. My associated duties as a compensation analyst for Chicago and Northwestern Railway and previously, for Inland Steel, give me the systematic expertise and necessary skills to become an immediate to your organization. In addition to these capabilities, I also have a firm understanding of the operational, organizational and planning skills associated with executive management responsibilities.

Because I firmly believe that it is necessary to possess both practical experience as well as theoretical knowledge, I have completed an MBA program in Human Resources and Management Information Systems.   I am now qualified for an opportunity that allows me to provide operational support with information systems. If given the opportunity, you will find me:
* Knowledgeable of the HAY job evaluation system
* Capable of developing and implementing an effective sales/incentive program
* Familiar with commission structures and able to conduct statistical analysis

I would appreciate the opportunity to discuss my skills and potential contributions in further detail at your convenience. Thank you for taking the time to review my background.

Sincerely,
Tom Gunderson

ELIZABETH HOLLENDONER
10415 Corfu Lane, Los Angeles, CA 90077
310-281-6184 • ehollendoner@hotmail.com

June 15, 2003
Dear Mr. Hall,

The recent listing on the UCLA website for the Student Affairs Officer V position (requisition 1797) caught my attention since it neatly fits my background and professional profile as noted in the attached resume.

Currently, I am the Director of Admissions and Student Recruitment for the Human Genetics Graduate Program at the University of Chicago. I accepted this role while completing a graduate degree in Managerial Communications from Northwestern University. As you can read, I am a former UCLA employee who worked in the David Geffen School of Medicine as a Student Affair Officer III. I truly enjoyed working at this fine institution and only moved to Chicago to complete my education.

I am now returning to Southern California in January and would like to continue applying my five-plus years of experience in student affairs.

Listed below are my qualifications relative to the duties of the Student Affairs Officer V position as noted in the job description.
- Successfully develop and execute all aspects of outreach recruitment and retention tactics of prospective graduate students.
- Provide both academic and personal consultation for a diverse student body.
- Execute university funding, financial aid and budget management.
- Five years experience at UCLA with in-depth knowledge of university policies and procedures; working knowledge of Graduate Admissions, Registrar's Office and Graduate Division.
- Supervision of administrative support staff.

Although it is hard to gauge how well a prospective employee will actually perform in his or her job once hired, it is worth noting that in each of my past roles I fully supported the vision, mission and goals of the department. If I am given the opportunity to handle the duties of Student Affairs Officer V at UCLA, I will contribute at a high level and will remain actively engaged with the same level of commitment as previously demonstrated

Attached is my resume for your review, which covers my experience and qualifications in detail. I am looking forward to the opportunity to further discuss how my skills and experience would assist the Graduate School of Education and Information Studies in meeting its goals. I would appreciate the opportunity to discuss my credentials with you.

Sincerely,

Elizabeth Hollendoner

DEBRA A. HOPKINS

642 N. Lombard   Oak Park, IL 60302   708-524-2054

I am submitting this letter and my resume in order to pursue the position of Executive Director of the Cook County Department of Corrections.

As I evaluated the opportunity to pursue this position, it became obvious that the CCDOC needs a strong leader who can direct the jail and it's inmate population into the 21st century. It is important to note that, given the opportunity, I will provide creative and realistic direction to achieve a successful tenure in the Office of Executive Director. My 23 years of progressive experience in the filed of corrections management has taught me the necessary concepts to motivate staff and to attack the dysfunctional nature of the jail population. I want to improve operational efficiency consistent with Illinois legal statutes pertaining to the criminal justice system as well as human rights protection.

My professional history at the CCDOC balances integration of practical, academic and administrative standards and procedures. As the first woman Supervisor in a male housing area, I developed the sensitivity and structural capabilities necessary to manage and direct a predominately male staff and jail population. As a Lieutenant and the Director of the Training Academy for four years, I developed and delivered relevant programs that educated new CCDOC Correctional Officers from DuPage, Kane and Will Counties, as well as supervisors and civilians. On a programmatic note, my specialized training from the National Institute of Corrections permitted me to introduce Hostage Behavior and Interpersonal Communications into the training curriculum.

My classroom participation as an instructor encouraged new employees to adapt to the self discipline and high standards that should be expected of an employee within the Cook County Sheriff's Department. My seven years of experience as the Superintendent of Division 3, afforded me the expertise to manage daily operations, develop and introduce programming and to secure funding for special programs from nontraditional sources. My public relations experience with radio and TV has allowed me to demonstrate to the general public a professional concern for their questions regarding our operations. On a more intimate level, public speaking to Churches and College classes, has strengthened my ability to communicate to disparate public groups the complex nature of CCDOC programs and policy issues.

As a public servant, it is my responsibility to lead, represent and respond professionally to my career responsibilities. In summation, these executive qualifications and management skills will allow me to continue to be an asset to the Cook County Department of Corrections. I look forward to the opportunity to discuss in further detail your needs and my specific qualifications for this position.

Sincerely,

Debra A. Hopkins

SHARON KELD

1360 N. Lake Shore Dr. #1404, Chicago, IL 60610 • 312-642-6966 • s_keld@hotmail.com

Commissioner Lois Weisberg
City of Chicago

Dear Commissioner Weisberg,

I am forwarding this resume to pitch my academic, business and promotional skills to you with the hopes that there is a need to add top staff to your world-class cultural and tourism marketing efforts. My dream is to help Chicago derive returns on their cultural and artistic investments by applying my strategic planning, project execution and product management expertise that has been tested in globally competitive business environments.

Although I am originally from the Queens borough of New York City, I have adopted this beautiful city and have become steeped in the lore, traditions and character that makes Chicago a stand-out amongst its municipal peers. I am a huge fan of so many of Chicago's destination advantages (host of two quality baseball teams, the push to lead the "Green/Livable City Movement", the best-in-class quality of the Art Institute and the stunning innovation of Millennium Park) that cheer-leading for the city comes naturally. Professionally, I have developed the creative expertise to build or launch new consumer offerings, generate revenue increases and expand market share. Additionally, I also have a firm grounding in the operational, organizational and administrative duties associated with marketing and promotional activities.

My desire is to help Chicago compete for mind-share, tourist dollars and the recognition that this progressive municipality deserves to enjoy. If, by chance, you are looking for a marketing professional with the vision and confidence to attain tangible business results and contribute to your initiatives, please consider the attached credentials.

Given the opportunity, you will find me dedicated, innovative and resourceful with a focus on adding value day in and day out. I would appreciate the opportunity to discuss present or projected needs that you are experiencing. Thank you for taking the time to review my background.

Sincerely,

Sharon Keld

Kathleen L. Lakin
3550 Lake Shore Drive #608, Chicago, IL 60657

_____

July21, 1993

Ms. Maureen Vaughn
CAMCO
1201 North Clark
Chicago, IL 60610

Dear Ms. Vaughn:

As per our conversation this morning concerning the position of a floating lease agent, I am sending you my resume. I have significant experience in the field of real estate with an extensive background in sales and administrative responsibilities. I find this work both mentally stimulating and personally rewarding, but it does not demand my full potential or capabilities. I am now seeking to continue a successful career that will allow me to demonstrate my abilities in the field of lease management.

In the last year and a half, while working at Stanmeyer, I completed three separate training courses pertaining to the field of real estate. These in combination with my real estate license courses and my practical experience in sales with Stanmeyer have given me the background and experience necessary to fulfill a position as a floating lease agent.

After receiving my resume, I hope you will find that I can become an immediate asset to your organization. I would appreciate the opportunity to discuss my skills and contributions to your company at your convenience.

Sincerely,

Kathleen L. Lakin

MICHAEL LEVIN
4647 Davis, Skokie, IL 60076   847-733-9294

October 8, 1996

Jerry Connell

ORACLE CORPORATION   ORACLE
601-657-0037

RE: Justice and Public Safety Sales Management Advertisement

As you consider my credentials, please allow me to briefly summarize salient points that should warrant serious consideration. Since graduating with a B.S. in Criminal Science in 1990, the summation of my experience within sales and sales management has taught me the necessary concepts to motivate staff and to supervise a complex array of team oriented projects. To capitalize on this history, my professional desire is to work for a software company that is involved with selling internet technology and data management tools.

As an account manager and sales trainer for Commerce Clearing House, I have developed and delivered relevant initiatives to create a successful sales territory that encompasses 5,000 accounts covered by 10 representatives that generate $15,000,000 in software sales annually (legal, safety, human resources and accounting). My ability to network and facilitate information exchanges between CEO'S, CFO's, Partners and Controllers has permitted our operation to achieve mission objectives. My particular strength lies in understanding how particular strategies and projects fit into the larger goals of the organization and prioritizing necessary action steps to achieve success.

My professional history balances integration of task management and administrative responsibilities that must be confronted on a daily basis. In my current sales/training role, I developed the insight necessary to direct a diverse work force. I am considered by my supervisors to be a hands-on manager with the personality and perseverance necessary to listen and be accessible to subordinates and peers alike. Given the opportunity you will find me able to communicate effectively at all corporate levels and enjoy working within team environments. In summation, these managerial qualifications and skills will allow me to become an immediate asset to your company.

I look forward to the opportunity to discuss in further detail your needs and my specific qualifications for this position.

Sincerely,

Michael Levin

ELIZABETH LYTLE
1320 Tamara Court, Waukegan, IL 60085 847-244-3275

May 10, 2002

Emily Terran
Operations Manager
Interior Garden Services, Inc.
20000 W. Fulton St.
Chicago, IL 60612

Dear Ms. Terran,

Thank you for your kind letter the other day noting the need for a qualified horticulturist to help your company continue to provide interior-scaping in Chicago. Needless to say your company's offer is exactly what I have been hoping to uncover and comes at a great time.

Currently I am in the garden section of a large retailer that is allowing me to apply my horticulture skills along with developing people skills, communication and marketing capabilities for their Waukegan property. Although I find this role challenging, it has always been a dream of mine to work within the interior setting.

I can say enthusiastically that if I am given the chance to contribute to your existing teams, I would work diligently to apply all of the skills I possess. Since I have a horticulture degree and associated certifications you can see that academically my background is fundamentally sound. I am also fortunate enough to have nearly ten years of professional experience working with demanding and discriminating clientele who relied on my subject matter expertise. In these capacities I took it as a matter of pride to always offer 110% to my employer as well as go the extra mile for my customer.

I hope that the enclosed resume will shed light on areas that can demonstrate a good fit with current openings that you are experiencing. I will be happy to follow-up with a phone call or am willing to wait for you to take the next step at your convenience.

Sincerely,

Elizabeth Lytle

ANDREW B. MELNICK
1422 W. George, Chicago, IL 60657 773-327-8337

November 6, 2000

Mike Scotty
President/CEO - **databasedads**
3110 N. Sheffield, Chicago, IL 60657

Dear Mike,

As I promised, here is a resume outlining my past seven years of selling, staff management and business development experience. The combination of account management skills along with entrepreneurial qualities will define how I might fit the Client Service Management role we discussed last week.

As the sole Account Manager for Infocomm I built client relationships which resulted in generating over $3 million in new revenues. The complex jobs that I produced for my account base of 40 clients lends itself nicely to the high volume traffic that databasedads experiences.

Success at Infocomm is a direct result of the challenges I met as owner of Magic and Vanity. This was a business that combined account development, direct marketing, P.R and sales. Building business revenues demanded a very proactive account development approach which included targeting Doctors of Oncology and Oncology Nurse Practitioners, hospitals and medical networks.

As sales grew, I hired a health care consultant to write a proposal that made us an approved vendor of durable medical equipment with Chicago based HMOs. At Magic and Vanity my wife and I hired and trained 10 employees whom we recruited to sell an extremely delicate product group (cancer patient prosthesis and wigs). Worth noting is that we trained the sales staff to treat their customers as an account executive would treat an account base. This meant that they conducted follow-up calls to confirm client satisfaction and to suggest new products.

Mike, I hope this adds illumination to our previous discussion. I realize that your primary concern is my limited residential real estate experience, but don't forget, I'm the son of a successful Realtor who wanted nothing more than to teach me all that he knew about the profession. I have a strong grasp of the real estate field and market place. I am extremely interested in helping databasedads succeed and if given the opportunity will deliver the results that are expected of an excellent Client Services Manager.

Sincerely,

Andrew Melnick

KEVIN M. MQNAGHAN

5615 N. Kedvale St., Chicago, IL 60646   (312) 583-8111

Myron D. Maurer
Director of Building Operations
MERCHANDISE MART PROPERTIES INC.
470 Merchandise Mart
Chicago, IL 60654

Dear Mr. Maurer:

I am forwarding this letter and a copy of my resume for your evaluation, on the referral Mr. Jim Reinke, who mentioned that you are currently looking for an experienced facility and maintenance manager for the Merchandise Mart.

Since beginning my career at Bankers Life and Casualty in 1976, I work each day to be a consistent, motivated and an organized manager .what I believe are the keys to my success. I you can tell from the enclosed resume, I have had the opportunity to work on a variety of assignments while holding the position of maintenance supervisor. I am eager to bring these skills and experiences to my next position. Because I believe in the philosophy of formal as well as practical training, I am currently in the process of finishing a certification program in refrigeration air conditioning and heating at the Coyne American Institute here in Chicago. By combining an extensive background with my education, I can come on board and become an immediate asset .with little or no additional training or supervision needed.

I would appreciate the opportunity to discuss my skills and contributions to your maintenance team, in more detail, during an interview. Thank you for reviewing my credentials.

Sincerely,

Kevin Moghnaghan

JAMES S. NOBIS
910 Elsie,   Melrose Park, IL 60160   708 -345- 4321

January 27, 1997

Lisa Martin
KMART
Fax: 847-202-2976

Dear Ms. Martin:

Since my responsibilities at White Hen have been completed as of last week (1/15/97), I am following up on our conversation regarding opportunities within your Pantry One Operations.

As a franchise owner/operator for White Hen, I worked daily to improve operations, streamline processes and strengthen relations with the many vendor representatives that serviced my territory. I developed efficient training procedures and operating controls to ensure the property remained profitable, well patronized and to act as a model within the district. The thrust of my responsibilities centered on balancing the internal demands of staff development with the ongoing need to increase revenue results and market presence by catering to the needs of the clientele. To orchestrate these operations, it was necessary for me to remain flexible in my strategic approach and to focus on attaining cohesion from my support staff. The results that I have obtained to date have been recognized by executive management and have justified their recommendations for formal recognition and awards.

Overall, the opportunity to apply entrepreneurial skills while honing management qualifications at White Hen challenged me on both a personal and professional level and leads me to desire even greater opportunities to develop these capabilities. Professionally, I am now interested in using my operational management, consumer marketing and strategic planning experience in a company that is focused on improving their sales operations, their service approach to the customer and product marketing strategies.

After you review my credentials, hopefully you will see that I can become an immediate asset to your organization. I appreciate your consideration of my background and look forward to discussing, in further detail, current opportunities.

Sincerely,

James S. Knobs

January 11, 2003

Julian Kanner
PRINCIPAL
John P. Altgeld School
1340 W. 71st St
Chicago, IL 60636

Dear Principal Kanner:

I am writing this letter in response to current vacancies at your school. I am currently certified in Elementary Education, K-9th grades. Presently I am a substitute teacher at Schneider Elementary school and have begun my search for a permanent teaching position for the '93-'94 school year.
My student teaching assignment at Gale Academy, in Chicago, included experiences with grade three, where my area of concentration was in English and Language Arts. I have also had experience working with a low reading group and was able to adapt seat work materials with a great deal of success.

Enclosed is my resume which highlights a few of my experiences and qualifications that have contributed to the development of my skills as a teacher. If you feel that my background could match any of your current open positions, please send me an application, and at your request, I will have a copy of my credentials sent for you to review.

Sincerely,

Susan Peagler (312) 764-5474

KATHERINE RICHARDSON
624 S. Austin, Oak Park, II 60304 708-386-9506

January 12, 2001

Nancy Dearhammer
Director
Lawndale Community School
3400 Grenshaw, Chicago, IL 60623

Dear Ms. Dearhammer,

Thank you for encouraging me to pursue the position of Business Manager for Lawndale Community School as it transitions into the L.E.A.R.N. Charter School. After speaking with you on the details of the position, it truly appears to be a good fit with my existing corporate background. I see specific relationship to my current work history in areas such as handling Accounts Receivable, Accounts Payable, Business Management, Community Marketing and Operation Control. These responsibilities, in one way or another, complement various roles I have held with ADP, Beckers and my Office Management position I had at Genesis.
What excites me about this opportunity is the possibility of continuing my involvement with the charter school systems. As you already know, my teaching duties with Lawndale is a continuation of working in the Charter arena since I first assisted the faculty at the New Orleans Charter School in 1998 by helping them to open the first Charter School in the city of New Orleans.

I think my strengths will be best utilized as I lead and execute annual fund - raising events with the community, the city and through grant applications. I know that my past seven years of business experience will allow me to speak to decision makers, community leaders and donors on a level that will give them confidence to support our programs and educational mission objectives.

Please rest assured that my efforts will focus not only on how I can secure necessary funding to support the school, but I will also look for ways to help the executive team with their projects whenever possible or when requested. I have been characterized by previous managers as a multi-tasking, multi-talented employee and find it personally rewarding to contribute to my peers and subordinates whenever possible.

Once again, I thank you for this wonderful opportunity to submit my credentials in pursuit of the position of L.E.A.R.N.S. Business Development Manager. If any additional information is needed please don't hesitate to call me directly.

Sincerely,

Katherine Richardson

KOSUKE SATO
845 West Washington, C-l, Oak Park, IL 60302, 708-848-6086

Ms. Colleen Walczyaowski
Arthur Andersen
Suite 1500 River Park Tower
333 West San Carlos Street San Jose, CA 95110-2710

Dear Ms. Walczyaowski,

As follow-up to a conversation I had with my friend Tsutom Ehara, and upon his recommendation, I would like to express an interest in pursuing a career as an auditor with Arthur Andersen. Because of the confidential nature of my employment search it is not feasible to hold an interview in Chicago, I would be delighted if you allow me the opportunity to visit the San Jose Office to learn more about employment opportunities. Since I am planning on getting together with Tsutom in the next two months, it might be a good time to meet for an interview then if your schedule permits.

As you can read in the resume, I recently completed my first year of employment with Ernst Young, which came right after the conclusion of a Master of Science in Accountancy (completed at the University ofIllinois in 1997).

My professional history includes participation on a number of corporate audits. My role as a staff member focused on providing support to our audit team as well as direct interaction with the client. What this has developed is the ability to multi-task, communicate effectively to a wide variety of professionals and meet extremely tight deadlines while maintaining accuracy. Prior to working for a big six accounting firm, I held positions that included an internship at Best Seller's Publishing in Minneapolis. At Best Sellers, I conducted research on Japanese publishing companies and marketed the rights to our catalog of books to them. Through all of these experiences I developed strong interpersonal and communication skills in business settings.

Overall, I believe Arthur Andersen is the place where I can best use my talents, skills and knowledge base. I hope that I have adequately conveyed my desire to meet with you. I would be grateful if you could spare your time during an interview and look forward to your response. Thank you for your consideration.

Sincerely,

Kosuke Sato

SHAWNA SPRECKELSEN 77 W. Huron #514 Chicago, IL 60610
312.915.4037

March 1, 1994

Lisa Abildskov
Human Resources
University or Utah Medical Center 421 Wakara Way, Suite 140
Salt Lake City, UT 84108
Re: Job # L.A. 3264

Dear Ms. Abildskov,

I am forwarding this letter and a current copy of my resume to your attention for consideration of the open position (as was noted by an H.R. representative when I called yesterday Monday, February 28) for a neonatal respiratory therapist.

Over the past 8 years I have gained significant experience as a registered respiratory care practitioner. As you will see, I have been working with Trav Corps since October '88 as a traveling therapist and have held a variety of challenging and exciting assignments that have sharpened my clinical skills. Although I find the traveling a rewarding experience and have learned to be innovative and flexible, I am now looking for a position that offers stability. My long term desire is to find an opportunity in Salt Lake City where I plan to settle. After reviewing my resume, I hope you will see that I can become an immediate asset to your hospital - with little or no additional training needed.

 You will find me:
O Adaptable, independent and resourceful
O Capable of handling increasingly demanding responsibilities and expectations

I would appreciate the opportunity to discuss my skills and potential contributions to your hospital at your convenience. Thank you for taking the time to review my background.

Shawna Spreckelsen

HENRY L. SULLIVAN III

430 S. Wisconsin St., Oak Park, IL 60302   708-383-3075   henrylsullivan3@attbi.com

Sharon Tylus
NORC Human Resources
1155 East 60th Street
Chicago, IL 60637

Dear Ms. Tylus,

I am forwarding this letter to pursue the opening for a Survey Specialist. The key reason for my interest in the position is that the job description so neatly fits my existing research background. As you can read in the resume, I successfully execute strategic research projects in a number of extremely competitive business environments. Professionally, my role as Research Associate for Stax has developed the skills and creative expertise needed to be an immediate contribution to your research team.

Currently, I am challenged as survey specialist to add value throughout the entire research process. Since Stax is a lean organization, each of the teams is organic in structure and member responsibilities. The point is that we all have a part in the initial design, survey refinement, and actual interview execution of testing our client's hypothesis. The result of this experience is a firm grounding across all associated duties in field based research.

Although I enjoy Stax, I am now looking for a new direction and another challenging opportunity that will demand my full potential. My desire is to align with NORC in order to add my vision to the excellent organizational program that is in place. This opportunity is ideal in that it will allow me to provide my experience in meeting demanding research expectations.

Given the opportunity to explain my work history in detail, you will find me dedicated and resourceful with a focus on meeting objectives. Thank you for taking the time to review my background.

Sincerely,

Henry Sullivan

November 8, 2000

Noel Massie
District Manager
UNITED PARCEL SERVICES
2301 Rose Street, Franklin Park, IL 60131

Dear Mr. Massie:

Thank you for allowing me to outline the qualifications that demonstrate my fit as a potential Operational Management Supervisor. I realize you must read numerous letters from staff who are looking for new opportunities, so I will summarize only key points that can help justify the promotion.

For your reference, I was made aware of the opening nearly two weeks ago when I was approached by my immediate supervisor, Lashandra McComb, along with Gary Groundwick the South Center Manager who both suggested and support my pursuit of the opening.

The best way to define my management capability is to outline elements of my duties that profile my professional strengths:

Experience	11 years over four positions. This includes being one of the first team members selected to staff the On-Call Air System.
Driver Training	I have had the opportunity to train three route drivers throughout my tenure.
Customer Service	As a driver, my professional focus was to directly handle customer needs on scheduling problems, service availability, and commitment times.
Sales	I have worked directly with clients and sales representatives on 3 specific occasions to convert them from the competition and build our package volume.
Efficiencies	My immediate manager asked me to help break out and restructure routes to ensure that we achieve effective time savings.

As a potential supervisor I want to emphasize that my dedication and loyalty to UPS explains why I work overtime without expecting compensation, I fix problems whenever the opportunity arises and I truly enjoy helping my peers as well as the management team to achieve our mission objectives. I look forward to hearing from you when time permits to discuss in further detail the OMS opportunity.

Sincerely,

Karen E. Thiesse

Cynthia L. Thorson

3222 N. Racine Ave.   Chicago, IL 60657   (312) 929-2177

April 4, 1995

Linda Wolff
McDONALD'S CORPORATION
McDonalds Plaza
Oak Brook, IL 60521

Dear Ms. Wolff,

I am forwarding this letter and a current copy of my resume in response to the NIRI listing that was posted as of January 26, stating your need for a qualified Manager of Investor Relations. Over the past five years I have gained significant experience in the areas of marketing, investor relations development (sell and buy sides), establishing corporate identity, directing media focus, etc. I find this work mentally stimulating and personally rewarding, and I am encouraged to search for an assignment that will allow me to continue a successful career in this field. After reviewing my resume I hope you see that I have the professional experience that will allow me to become an immediate asset on your staff.

Since receiving an MBA from Northwestern's J.L. Kellogg Graduate School of Management, I have kept a busy itinerary, handling responsibilities as the Manager of Investor Relations for Chicago and North Western Railway and previously, as an Associate Media Planner for Sears National Catalog. At CNW, I had the opportunity to build profitable, ongoing relationships with a variety of buy-side and sell-side parties. I also managed all critical investor communications and maintained senior management coordination to ensure consistent information dissemination. At Sears, I focused on developing product marketing, strategic planning and staff coordination efforts. My current goal is to find a position that will continue to allow me to continue demonstrating creative capabilities and communication skills.

I would appreciate the opportunity to discuss my skills and potential contributions, in further detail, at your convenience. Thank you for taking the time to review my background.

Sincerely,

Cynthia L. Thorson

Shawn Walls
5451 S. Cornell
Chicago, IL 60615
February *25,* 1998

Aon Corporation
14th Floor KP *-4505*
123 N. Wacker Drive
Chicago, IL 60606

Dear Human Resource Manager:

I am applying for the position of compliance analyst that was advertised on Jan 12, 1998 with the placement service at Roosevelt University. The position seems to fit very well with my education, experience, and career interests.

In addition to my education received from Harold Washington College and Roosevelt University, I have bad the opportunity to intern at The Chicago Corporation. In the accounting department, this position allowed me to strengthen my analytical skills. I accepted assignment in the asset management group, which provided interpersonal relationship and exposure. Also, the Conseco Companies diversified healthcare insurance department and its Risk Management Group provided additional work experience.

This is to say that I believe the experience and professional stature that I present to you for consideration are those practical and sound in nature. As you will note in the enclosed resume, my skills and abilities could be put to good use by your corporation.

Would you please consider my request for a personal interview to discuss further my qualifications and to learn more about this opportunity? I shall call you next week to see if a meeting can be arranged. Should you need to reach me, please feel free to call me at (773) 288-0824. If I am no in, please leave a message on my answering machine and I will return your call within a day.

Thank you for your consideration. I look forward to talking with you.

Sincerely,

Shawn Walls

MARTIN **OLIVER WATSON**

169 Watson Rd., Fairport, NY 14450
Home: 716-388-9079

November 12, 1996

Starbucks Coffee Company
Mr. Scott Bedberry
Senior Vice President of Sales and Marketing
Marketing Department S-MK3
P.O. Box 34067
Seattle, Washington, 98 124-1067

Dear Scott:

Congratulations on the continuing success of Starbucks Coffee Company. From what I've learned about your company, you have aggressive plans for future growth. I would like to help in achieving your goals.

It seams to me that the grocery and grocery wholesale market segments offer Starbucks Coffee Company excellent potential for high volume sales of both liquid and bean coffees. If your future plans include continued expansion into the grocery segment, then I would like to discuss my qualifications with you.

My areas of expertise include new product and new market development in the grocery wholesale grocer and food service sectors. The attached resume reflects ten years of experience and success launching and growing new products in these market channels. Additionally, I have sales experience and contacts throughout the North American grocery channel.

My current projects bring me to Seattle occasionally and I would like to meet with you at your convenience. In fact, I will be in Seattle on Wednesday, November 13th and could meet you then.

Please contact me and let me know when you are available.

Sincerely,

Marty Watson

Joseph W. Washington

8317 S. Burnham, Chicago, IL 60649   773-375-1633 (hm.) • 773-535-4020 (wk.)

Bulletin: #114
Cook County Dept. of Corrections
Alternative High School
Principleship

Mr. Thomas J. Doyle
DIRECTOR, DEPARTMENT OF HUMAN RESOURCES
1818 West Pershing Road, 6C(c)
Chicago, IL 60609

Dear Mr. Doyle,

While writing this letter of application, I spent much time considering issues surrounding the opportunity to work with men at Cook County D.O.C. As I reviewed my qualifications, it became clear to me that my professional background matches that needs of this institution. As you can see from my employment history, I have developed an ability to lead, coordinate and ensure the delivery of academic standards necessary to successfully comply with a school's mission of preparing men and women to thrive within and make valid contributions to our society.

I am now looking for a principalship opportunity that will allow me to continue balancing the varied goals of motivating, challenging and incenting students, as well as the teaching staff, to achieve their full potential. My ultimate goal is to participate as a key member of a professional administrative team that is focused on positively impacting the lives of their student population. After reviewing my resume, I hope you see that my personal dedication and ability to foster positive team dynamics, as well as efficiently manage resources, will allow me to successfully perform the responsibilities of principal and to become an immediate asset to this school.

On a personal level, in order to balance academic qualifications with practical experience, please note my completion of a Masters of Arts in Education Administration and the current pursuit of a Education Doctorate. These programs emphasize developing proactive, participatory educational professionals skilled in behavior modification as well as an awareness of social and multicultural issues that confront today's student population. As a teacher, my professional focus emphasizes student/teacher contact and uses a results oriented curriculum style that institutionalizes quality and integrates technology.

I would appreciate the opportunity to discuss my skills and potential contributions to your school at your convenience.

Sincerely,

Joseph W. Washington

SCOTT M. WEBBER

555 W. Madison Street, Apt. 1504,   Chicago, IL 60661   (312) 879-1150

Mr. Ron Wolf
General Manager
GREENBAY PACKERS
P.O. Box 10628, Greenbay, WI 54307-0628

Dear Mr. Wolf:

I am forwarding this letter and copy of my resume on the recommendation of Ms. Jeanne Bruette. Sir, I realize you are a busy executive and time is of the essence, so please allow me to be direct and openly honest.

My resume states that I am a graduate of the University of Wisconsin-Green Bay. It does not state that my heart and soul belongs in Green Bay - which it does. It does not mention that the Packers are in my blood or that the phrase fanatical fan best describes my level of enthusiasm. Mr. Wolf, I find myself in the precarious position of wanting something so badly that I will accept any opportunity that the Packer organization can find that will allow me to help the club.

I realize your organization is highly regarded across the NFL, that you have positioned the team to be a leader and to be a Super Bowl contender. I would like to congratulate you for the recognition you received as the NFL Executive of the Year. Although we have not yet met, I can say that we share a commonality of character traits:
☑ Dedication - 110% effort in every assignment.
☑ Excellence - Measured by tangible factors, sealed by my word as a man and a professional.
☑ Loyalty   - In all situations, unequivocal commitment that does not waver.

During my career, I've focused on building an excellent track record that increased company revenues, improved profitability and exceeded corporate goals. At Quantum Chemical, I generate $30 million in annual sales which represents one of the company's three largest territories. I'm comfortable handling substantial responsibilities and enjoy working for a company that demands a team commitment from the staff.

My ultimate goal is to establish myself as a dependable and contributing factor to the ongoing success of the Green Bay Packers. Mr. Wolf, I realize that without the opportunity to put a face with a name, my desire to work for your staff is not possible, therefore I would like to have a few minutes of your time to discuss in person potential assignments that might be available currently or in the near future.

Sincerely,

Scott M. Webber

Lionel Sweeny, Jr.
Director, Human Resources
MOTOROLA
Network Solutions Sector – North American Region
1301 E. Algonquin Road – IL02-SH4-Schaumburg, IL 60196

Dear Mr. Sweeny,

I am forwarding this letter and resume to your attention in order to pursue currently available executive opportunities with Motorola in the Chicagoland region. As you can see my career has focused on human resources and organizational development with a strong background in clinical and organizational psychology.

My recent emphasis was to participate on a team of specially selected mangers with the mission of combining two large business units into one group known as General Business Services prior to the merger between Ameritech and SBC. My team's function was to combine the two HR units into one entity. Overall, the successful conclusion of this project resulted in gaining efficiencies that netted $68 million. The application of organizational development and human resources development programs combined to ensure that SBC could actually achieve such substantial savings.

In my position as Director of Shared Business Leadership Development Services, my task was to improve the operation of all 17 business units through the use of change management processes in three specific areas: Foundations of Leadership, Project Management and Performance Management. I accomplished this task by maximizing resources and by removing the duplication of platforms that had the same business objectives. At the same time, I created and executed a Shared Leadership Development Program to accelerate the development of managers throughout Ameritech. This program ensured that participants could identify their roles in leading and driving change to execute Ameritech's strategic agenda. In addition, I designed curriculums that would enable corporate to achieve greater process improvements. The result led to over 500 managers being trained through the Foundations of Leadership program

As a byproduct of my work in change management, I was often asked by VPs, General Mangers and Directors to provide various kinds of interventions around conflict management and change management with many of their leadership groups. This work frequently involved coaching senior leaders through a variety of leadership issues.

The result of a career dedicated to organizational and leadership development has led to writing a book, *Conflict Management for the Professional OD Consultant*, to be published by Jossey Bass Publishing in the near future. I hope this information sheds enough light on my areas of competence to justify further discussions regarding the possibility of bringing these skills to Motorola. I look forward to speaking with you in the near future.

Sincerely,

Reginald Winston

MICHAEL WOLFE

2427 Reynolds Dr., Ottawa, IL 61350 815-433-6508 michael.wolfe@exeloncorp.com

June 7, 2001

Requisition: 200820
Title: Contract Administrator
Unit: Exelon Power Team

I am forwarding this resume in response to the posting for Contract Administrator on the Exelon Power Team. My interest in the position stems from a desire to continue supporting the critical business decisions impacting contracting, regulatory/legal compliance, and finance issues that impact Exelon's ability to continue to go forward profitably.

The summation of my experience focuses on leading change management, operational and special projects where the end goal is cost-control oriented. Because the projects are spread across a spectrum of issues, it is worth noting that a central focus was to ensure stability, continuity and minimize operational downtime.

As a professional, I make it a personal goal to execute corporate directives in a manner where results are measurable, the quality demonstrates ingenuity and attention to detail expresses my integrity. In other words, throughout my career I have worked daily to improve my effectiveness and have learned that hard work, and dedication are the keys to my success.

As a Technical Manager/Physicist, I have developed and implemented programs, procedures, and operational processes that impacted the efficiency and profitability of Exelon. I found this work professionally challenging and mentally stimulating and it challenged me to meet my full potential. I think the role of Contract Administrator will fit my business objectives and allow me to excel by applying the management and analytical skills gained from the Masters of Science in Finance.

I appreciate your consideration of my background and look forward to discussing, in detail, the responsibilities associated with possible positions on your staff.

Sincerely,

Michael Wolfe

BELEN ZANGRILLI
747 S. Euclid Ave., Oak Park, Illinois 60304
708 848-8689

March 22, 2001

Ms. L. Richards, HR/DCS
UHC
Spring Rd., Suite 700
Oakbrook, IL. 60523

Dear Ms. L. Richards:

Thank you for taking the time to consider my credentials. I hope to convey from my background a thorough understanding of the methodology, principles and support activities associated with becoming a Nurse. My insight to assisting students, designing curriculum and delivering lectures in Medical-Surgical Nursing compliments a background of 20+ years in staff nursing. It might be worth noting that as a nurse educator, I have received a high number of positive student surveys as feedback. This fact should communicate my desire to go beyond what is normally expected in order to prepare students to be effective in the modern medical environment.

Educationally, my focus has had a strong emphasis toward administration, research in medical nursing ethics, and psychiatric counseling. Throughout my academic and occupational experiences, I consistently choose roles that expand my understanding of how to relate as an educator, researcher, and counselor to individuals from cultures outside of my own as well as develop managerial and organizational skills.

Due to these experiences, I am able to teach in varied environments and have the ability to connect with a vast array of personalities. I believe that my knowledge and strong stance on education, research, counseling and client advocacy will make me an excellent candidate for your organization.

I also believe that it is important to recognize that students develop best when they are encouraged to excel individually as well as within a team environment. I understand that instructors should have the proven ability to provide effective, efficient, and creative health care instruction. Ultimately, when teachers and students are in harmony, the objectives of the institution are achieved. I hope this conveys my potential to participate and to become a contributing staff asset.

Sincerely,

Belen Zangrilli

December 19, 2003

Pfizer Inc.,
425 N. Martingale Road, Suite 900
Schaumburg, IL 60173

Post ID: 1013096

Dear Dave,

I am very interested in the Institutional Healthcare Representative position. I have eight years of proven success in the medical device/pharmaceutical industry. I have prior experience from my Milex career, working with pharmacy, purchasing and residency programs. My career path at Searle allowed me the opportunity to get Ambien on formulary on the South-side hospitals.

My Arthritis and Pain Specialty position at Pharmacia allowed me access to work with Specialists and Residents at the following teaching institutions: Northwestern, University of Chicago and Loyola. Currently I am on the PD2 division working for Tony Hirschtritt. I am responsible for the Loop, Northwestern, St. Joe's Hospital and Lincoln Park Hospital.

I feel I have the right leadership, positive energy, competitive drive, communication and teamwork skills to help raise the bar for any district, lat or region. I can adapt readily to new environment and welcome opportunities at the chance to grow and develop new relationships, skills and talent. I would like to have a personal interview with you. Thank you for your consideration.

Sincerely,

Kristin Zaun

CHAPTER 4
GENERAL COVER LETTERS

JOHAN ARNBERG

1923A N. Howe St., Chicago, IL 60614
312-266-0120 (Home) • 847-228-5600 (Office)

In order to secure support during my current career transition, I have become aware that your firm has expertise with international search assignments that would fit my professional background. I am interested in a position that combines my background in strategic planning, project oversight, and client retention efforts within globally competitive business environments. Professionally, my management responsibilities as the President of Pullmax, and previously, as the Sales/Marketing Manager Worldwide at Pressmaster, have developed the executive skills and creative expertise needed to generate revenue increases and successfully expand international sales territories. Additionally, I also have a firm grounding in the operational, organizational and planning duties associated with direct marketing and sales activity.

Although I truly enjoy my current position, I am now looking for another challenging opportunity that will demand my full potential. My desire is to realign myself with a company that is competing for an increased global market share and looking for a senior executive with the vision and the confidence to attain strong revenue results, implement cost management initiatives and build team cohesion. The ideal opportunity will allow me to direct marketing/sales efforts for a company committed to rapid expansion or is repositioning itself to compete in new markets.

Given the opportunity, you will find me dedicated, innovative and resourceful with a focus on building a top level staff that are prepared to win business. I would appreciate the opportunity to discuss present or projected needs that you are experiencing. Thank you for taking the time to review my background.

Sincerely,

Johan Arnberg

JADE CHOU
850 N. Lake Shore Dr., #1708, Chicago, IL 60611, 312-482-2358
E-mail: w-chou@nwu.edu

Thank you for allowing me to forward this letter and a current copy of my resume in order to pursue associate opportunities within your law firm. My desire is to correlate academic qualifications, in both the legal and business management arenas, with practical experience that I gained when working for the highly reputable international trademark/patent law firm of Saint Island in Taiwan.

As you can see, my personal and professional background has a heavy international orientation: Cultural awareness of: Asian/American/UK/German national idiosyncrasies; Linguistic comfort with English, German and Mandarin Chinese; as well as Business knowledge of - Asian, U.S. corporate practices. This knowledge will allow me to become an immediate impact in support of your firm's litigation efforts.   T o maximize my full professional potential, education and business skills, I am interested in a position that will capitalize on my knowledge of the Asian marketplace.

Over the past five years, during and subsequent to graduating from college, you can see that I have kept a busy itinerary handling challenging professional, academic, and social responsibilities. My main strengths lie in the ability to remain flexible and adapt to corporate cultures in various business settings. In summation, I have learned the fundamental skills, and developed my creative capabilities to become an immediate corporate asset.

You will find me dedicated, innovative and resourceful, a professional that is determined to be a top performer and capable of handling increased responsibilities. I would appreciate the opportunity to discuss my skills in further detail at your convenience. Thank you for taking the time to review my background.

Sincerely,

Jade Chou

111 E. Chestnut #32A, Chicago, IL 60611

This letter and resume are in response to the opening for a Regional Sales Manager – Business Performance Management Practice. As I read the description of the qualifications, my interest in the opportunity grew since the role neatly fits my background and skill set. As you can read in the resume, my sales and business development experience includes the tactical ability to execute direct marketing efforts, close technical sales, manage senior level relationships as well as the strategic ability to adopt dynamic technologies to large-dollar enterprise deals targeting the Fortune 500.

Although I find many similarities from your job posting and my skills, I pinpoint only key attributes for the sake of brevity. Fundamentally, my life's work is more than a job, it is a passion for sales that drives me to excel. I am a quick study on industry characteristics and commit large amounts of personal time to stay aware of emerging trends to capture new business opportunities. I constantly monitor market transitions, stay abreast of competitive pressures and analyze client driven demands.   The combination of having worked in divergent industries as a senior account executive allows me to maximize potential, demonstrate multi-tasking capabilities and will help me become an immediate asset to your existing team.

At Oracle, I quickly transitioned from HRIS sales to where I now manage a group of Named-Accounts that generate over $4,000,000 annually. In this role, I balanced a busy schedule by providing client service support, directing sales development efforts and executing corporate business plans. I have learned to focus on remaining flexible while allocating personal resources efficiently to maximize sales potential.

Overall, you will find that I am innovative, resourceful and capable of handling all levels of development responsibilities; in other words, I desire to remain a key-contributing factor of a company's revenue objectives. Thank you for taking the time to review my background.

Sincerely,

Kathy Cipriani

SANFORD A. COHEN
8926 N. Greenwood Ave., #121, Niles, IL 60714   773-792-6786
sanco@ix.netcom.com

The purpose for contacting you personally is to reestablish networking links as I continue a career in the music industry. More specifically, I am pursuing new opportunities in radio or record label promotions. Briefly stated, I am looking to integrate the extensive experience and contacts I gained from past promotions of record labels including Chicago's Underground Construction. During this tenure, I helped build public awareness of the producer's product in Chicago which in turn successfully built market share and increased unit sales. While working with UC, I also had the opportunity to participate in the New York Seminar as well as the Winter Music Conference at Miami Beach, Florida.

When hired to conduct free-lance promotional work for Star Bound Records out of L.A. the focus was on KC and The Sunshine Band's mega mix and Big Band Swing remix. I also was retained to do independent promotional work for Gold Star Promotions, based in West L.A. In this effort we built presence in the Midwest for Vicki Sue Robinson's single "House of Joy" that was produced by Junior Vasquez for Pagoda of New York and released by Drive Entertainment out of L.A, California. Most recently, I have been retained by Crossover Entertainment to participate in a mass market campaign targeting dance stores in Metro Chicago for three techno compilation CD's.

As a promoter, I became adept at developing relationships in order to help producers with diverse style and creative talent expand their acceptance at the club, radio and retail levels. The unique trait that distinguishes my approach to working with the client is the pride I take in remaining flexible and adaptable in meeting varied personal demands.

My chief ability is to create promotions that are both unique and provocative yet maintain wide audience accessibility. The ultimate goal is to link the artistic aesthetic to the potential consumer's subjective tastes and sensibilities. I emphasize a sincere commitment to meeting the client's expectations by maintaining accountability throughout the entire promotional process.

Please contact me at the number above so that we can continue to discuss how I can be of assistance to you in the future.

Sincerely,

Sanford A. Cohen

SANFORD A. COHEN

8926 N. Greenwood Ave., #121, Niles, IL 60714   773-792-6786

sanco@ix.netcom.com

I am sending this letter to your academic institution in order to pursue current teaching opportunities in your language arts, literature and speech department. Although this is my professional teaching focus, I also want to state that my extensive Chicago area drama experience will allow me to participate in your theater program. In addition to this, if needed, my coaching experience will allow me to get involved with your basketball and baseball teams. After working in corporate America for the past dozen plus years, I have decided the best way to use my knowledge and serve the community is to bring my leadership capabilities and an understanding of interpersonal communication skills back to the classroom.

My desire is to combine experience with developing operational and administrative procedures with demonstrable teaching skills. As a teacher, I would like to continue building rapport with young people, while maintaining an encouraging and disciplined classroom learning environment. It has been said that my work ethic is an inspiration to my peers and an encouragement to my managers. I consider my perseverance and enthusiasm to share knowledge the keys to my professional success.

My interest in pursuing a position with a preparatory boarding school is not only to continue a career that I love, but also to complement my experience of having personally attended Culver Naval School (where I achieved a certificate for completing a highly acclaimed Naval Training Program). In addition to Culver, I am a graduate of Miami Military Academy. At Miami Military, the experience was so impressive and rewarding, that it was natural to send my own child to continue the legacy. So the third college prep school that I have been affiliated with was Howe Military School, where I sent my youngest daughter to learn dedication, loyalty and a sense of discipline as well as to become a good citizen. The culmination is that she has developed into a young lady that desires to contribute to society by joining the US Air Force. Overall this has convinced me of the continuing value that such an education affords.

I would like to note that as a teacher, I have implemented the whole child teaching approach, where I consider the physical, emotional, social and intellectual state of the pupil. In addition, by integrating study techniques such as, cooperative learning, I ensure each child's chance to succeed. As a modern teacher, I realize that I must be multifaceted and capable of performing in a variety of roles, including providing assistance with extracurricular activities.

I would appreciate an interview to discuss my qualifications at a suitable time. Thank you for your consideration of me as a future educator in your fine institution.

Cordially,

Sanford A. Cohen

DAVID A. JAYSON
867 Honeysuckle Ave., West Chicago, IL 60185, 630-231-3482

davejayson@sbcglobal.net

Dear Mark Thompson,

I am seeking your search support to market my Facilities Management background to a large or mid-sized organization needing a seasoned professional who possesses expertise in strategic planning, project leadership, and contractor management efforts at a regional or national level. Ideally, a role that allows me to combine my expertise in strategic planning, project leadership, and contractor management at a regional or national level.

My responsibilities, currently as Facilities Property Administrator with *Bridgestone/Firestone* and previously as Area Facilities Manager at **7-Eleven** and Corporate Facilities Manager at **FTD, Inc.'s Headquarters** allowed me to develop the leadership skills and creative expertise needed to optimize cost structures, manage wide-spread contractor relations and deliver bottom line results. As you can see in the attached resume, I am also well grounded in operational, organizational and planning duties associated with launching enterprise-level project initiatives.

Although the challenges at Bridgestone/Firestone have extended my knowledge of the facility management role (I oversee 25% of all US facilities), I think that the time is good to seek a Director or VP level assignment either in Chicago or elsewhere (for the right opportunity, I am geographically flexible). Since I thrive in dynamic corporate cultures, the company type is not as important as their need to hire managers who possess the vision to implement cost management initiatives and build team cohesion.

It may be obvious to mention this, but if I am given the opportunity, I will present in a manner that reflects positively on your firm's ability to recruit top-level management talent. Let's discuss present or projected searches you are conducting. Thank you for reviewing my background.

Sincerely,

David Jayson

GRACE YUN KIM

3452 Salem Walk AG, Northbrook IL 60062 847-298-7545

I am forwarding this letter and resume to pursue web design and support opportunities with your company. For *3* years, I've helped Windy City Software, a small, leading-edge technology-consulting firm in Chicago that specializes in original program creation, implementation and c-commerce. Since I will be moving to California in May, I hope to find a short or long-term consulting opportunity or a position on a technical project team that will allow me to integrate my IT skills.

At Windy City, my experience started as their technical writer and then progressed into that of web designer and web site manager. As you can see from my background, I successfully launched numerous projects to initiate the company's web presence. The project orientation of this experience allowed me to sharpen team leadership, communication and problem solving skills that will allow me to adapt quickly to a new technology culture.

Professionally, my leadership values and decision-making skills have been tested across a diverse rage of duties. Because we had so many clients and a diverse set of projects to work on, I was able to demonstrate that 1 can learn quickly, possess good communication skills and work will with my team members. At Windy City, I remained focused and helped the company meet budget and schedule constraints by executing each project phases on time. Really, the fact is that I enjoy working on the technology that we designed. As an HTML programmer, I continuously hone my skills by networking with other web designers through the Internet and explore new ideas that eventually work their way into my programming. I see the role of Web Designer as a mandate to remain adaptable and learn how to apply continuously evolving technologies. I see no limits as to my abilities and have made it a personal challenge to create technology landmarks that bring value to the entire net community. Technologically, I'm detail oriented and can provide the multi-tasking support that is needed to work with many projects simultaneously.

The summation of my experience is a successful track record that has improved daily operations for our company and for our clients. I would appreciate the opportunity to discuss your information technology needs and objectives at your convenience. Thank you for taking the time to review my background.

Sincerely,

Grace Yun Kim

JEFF KRAMER

kramer_jeff@yahoo.com 6158 Coventry Ct., Carpentersville, IL 60110 • 847.836-8020

I am interested in pursing selling or sales management opportunities, preferably in a role that will apply my strategic business building experience gained over the past 13 years as an account executive, sales representative and channel sales manager.

For the past two years, I have muti-tasked between completing an MBA at a top ranked institution while handling the complex responsibilities as CardSmart's AE for their Chicago office. During this period, I've developed keen insight to business from sound academic instruction DePaul offers while continuing to apply practical skills on numerous consulting sales projects. This balance of business theory complemented by business practice allows me to quickly transition into a dynamic corporate culture and ensures that I am an immediate team asset.

Since the projects that I worked on are broad, it is worth noting that my contributions typically segment as follows:

Analytical
- Data analysis via interviews and line observations to determine core industry variables.
- Evaluating existing standard operating procedures to gauge effectiveness and suggest enhancements.

Strategic
- Developing business strategies to penetrate new markets or build sales distribution channels.
- Creating training tools and incentive programs to improve productivity and customer satisfaction.

Management
- Implementing system changes within the workplace.
- Integrating change management initiatives to ensure smooth transition throughout the corporation.

I work independently or as a member of larger teams with equal success and use leadership skills to motivate staff, peers and client contacts alike. Overall, I relentlessly pursue all viable avenues to identify resources and provide solutions for my clients.

I believe Wm. Meier & Associates requires individuals with strong interpersonal skills, ethical standards and technological awareness and appreciate your consideration.

Sincerely,

Jeff Kramer

WILLIAM J. KRISS

5 Oak Brook Club Dr., Oak Brook, IL 60523 630-842-9141 • wjkriss@att.net

I am forwarding this letter to pursue a senior executive role where I am challenged to continue providing management leadership in meeting the fiscal, operational and profit goals of the corporation I serve. As you can read from the resume, I thrive in an environment where I am expected to attain results within a globally competitive marketplace.

Although my career spans 25 years, a common thread that ties together each role are the contributions on both sides of the business building equation. During early stages of corporate development, I am deeply involved with the due diligence process to consummate an acquisition (i.e., cash flow analysis, evaluating financial soundness and interacting with the representatives at the businesses we were interested in buying) later, as the business is ramping up, I focus on operational efforts as the President or CEO responsible for rationalizing the operation and capturing the efficiencies that lead to sustainable profits.

The summation of my experience is a successful track record of executing activities as both a team leader and project manager. The proven success across a variety of business settings have refined my professional strengths and ensure that I can make correct decisions in the heat of conflict, under competitive pressure or in the board room. I am now looking for a career opportunity that allows me to continue balancing both the human and capital aspects of business. To attain these goals, I have concentrated on a flexible entrepreneurial style that is:

- Adaptable to diverse corporate cultures, dedicated, innovative and resourceful
- Capable of directing management teams and developing strategic alliances
- Highly energetic and capable of handling increasingly demanding challenges

I would appreciate the opportunity to discuss my skills and potential contributions to compliment your company. Thank you for taking the time to review my background.

Sincerely,

William J. Kriss

MARK ORENSTEIN

1034 N. Hayes, Oak Park, IL 60302 708-848-6673

I am forwarding this letter and copy of my resume in order to pursue a sales management or a sales-team leadership position that will allow me to continue capitalizing on a history of strategic sales planning, project oversight, and technology management expertise within competitive business environments. As you can read in the attached resume, during the past 14 years, I have developed business expertise as an entrepreneur where I built an $8,000,000 business from a $15,000 investment as well as in the role of general manager for two retail operations that needed a turn-around expert. My understanding of how to market products and services as well as build sales relationships with a diverse clientele has achieved successful competitive advantages for the companies I have led and should demonstrate that I can be an immediate asset with your company.

As a manager, my decision making skills have been tested and formed across a diverse rage of responsibilities which taught me how to balance both the human and capital aspects of business. The practical nature of my work history has sharpened my leadership, communication and problem solving capabilities. In summation, my career is built on seeking new challenges, developing realistic goals and achieving results.

On a personal level, my emphasis is to motivate staff while promoting a positive outlook throughout the company. To attain these goals, I concentrate on a flexible management style that is adaptable, innovative and resourceful. I would appreciate the opportunity to discuss my skills and potential contributions at your earliest convenience. Thank you for taking the time to review my background.

Sincerely,

Mark Orenstein

ROBERT A. PEACOCK

P.O. Box 721123, Roselle, IL 60172) 630-430-5559 ⊠ rangers90@msn.com

I am seeking a telecommunications management, project management, or help desk opportunity. Since I recently graduated with a Bachelor of Science in Telecommunications Management where the program of study had a strong emphasis on computer networking skills with project management and team work, I hope to find a position working in a collaborative environment. Due to a military background, I have been challenged to contribute as both a team leader as well as team member.

In the Army, I was considered by my superiors and peers as someone who could be trusted and was able to innovate solutions during complex assignments. I realize that I have to prove myself in a new position and am eager to have the chance to demonstrate that I am persistent and dedicated, yet maintain a flexibility that allows me to adapt to any situation.

My personal guarantee: If given a chance to work for you, I will perform at an exceptional level and will spend the necessary effort on my own time necessary to learn, grow and achieve your goals.

In addition, I am willing to travel and relocate. I also am willing to handle a variety of tasks no matter how large or small, in other words, please consider my application for any opening that is within the technical arena.

I have enclosed my resume for your review. I look forward to meeting with you so that we can further discuss your exciting opportunity and my related qualifications. I look forward to discussing in further detail your needs and how I can contribute.

Sincerely,

Robert Peacock

LADA PROKOFIEVA
1639 RIDGE AVE, #10-1 Evanston, IL 60201   (847) 492 9579

I am sending this letter and copy of my resume in order to pursue international executive or consulting assignments that fit my professional background. I am interested in a position that combines my strategic planning, project oversight, and business development efforts within globally competitive environments. Professionally, my management duties as a Fund Manager, a Corporate Director and a C.F.O. have developed the executive skills and creative expertise needed to generate revenues and successfully expand international operations. Additionally, I have a firm grounding in the organizational and planning duties associated with marketing and sales activities.

As you can see, I moved to the US in 1996 and have used my time to polish English language skills as well as acclimatize myself to the American business style. Because of the global village aspect of international business, my executive management expertise and broad contact base in the former Soviet Union should become advantageous to any company that is considering to improve their presence in that region. I want to align myself with a company that is looking for a senior executive with the vision and the confidence to attain strong revenue results, implement cost management initiatives and build team cohesion. The ideal opportunity will allow me to impact marketing/sales efforts for a company that is repositioning itself to compete in these new markets.

Given the opportunity, you will find me dedicated, innovative and resourceful with a focus on building a top level staff. I would appreciate the opportunity to discuss present or projected needs that you are experiencing at your convenience. Thank you for taking the time to review my background.

Sincerely,

Lada Prokofieva

Dear Church Leadership,

The central theme of my life is to understand and meet the needs of people. This passion that continuously stirs me to action has three components and is best exemplified as I interact with individuals on a daily basis.

- Firstly, because many people are struggling with inner hopelessness and lack of motivation, I plant seeds of hope-filled confidence as I counsel, teach and lead small groups. Often the result a shift in perspective will energize a person to view their life as meaningful and purposeful.

- Secondly, my goal is to encourage and assist individuals in discovering their personal and positive qualities. Authentic and affirming words are the foundation for a healthy self esteem and outlook toward the future.

- Thirdly, my life's passion is to offer direction towards new paths of life. There is difficulty oftentimes to step onto fresh paths of living when our personal lives are in the midst of unexpected troubles.

As a staff member of a large church, I have various opportunities to speak with those who need to turn a corner and to help them look forward instead of remaining immobilized in the past.

Through my years of education, social service, counseling and pastoral care, one of the greatest joys has been observing people as they discover their new found strength of motivation, future outlook, and direction towards a fresh life path.

My sincere desire for employment with your organization is to have opportunities to influence and interact with people. The experience, skills and education that I have developed and sharpened over the years is presently a benefit in the lives of many people. My staff responsibilities, along with teaching, counseling, hospital visitation, and community building has contributed greatly in the development of my intense passion and vision for helping people.

As you review my resume for consideration, references will be provided upon request.

Sincerely,

Ava M. Perry

GERALD J. SAWEIKIS

8440 West 122nd Place, Palos Park, IL 60464,   708-361-2740   gerrys@orbitel.com

I am forwarding my credentials to pursue an Information System/Technology management opportunity. As a professional, I build IS/IT programs to systematically improve a corporation's operational effectiveness. As a business entrepreneur, I design software products that are strong enough to go to market, and then lead the sales efforts to attain steady revenue growth and healthy profit margins.

As a knowledge leader and CIO, I've led strategic technology projects where team management and problem solving was executed at the rapid pace of changing technology. As a businessman, I choose staff that can adapt to change quickly and use technology to capture a competitive business edge. As a business owner of a technology firm, I designed and programmed all of my systems in COBOL for a mainframe and then converted everything to a PC when this technology was feasible. Once the system was converted I successfully marketed it throughout Europe and Asia.

The summation of my experience is a career built by developing realistic goals and achieving results. My ideal job would be with an international company with a technology product to market, hopefully in the securities/commodities/investment area. My job function would be to support the existing client base, bring in new clients and interface with the developers regarding existing and new customer needs/requests based on current and new technologies.

As a CIO, I've led technology projects where team management and problem solving was executed at the rapid pace of changing technology. I choose staff who can adapt to change quickly and use technology to capture a competitive business edge. As a business owner of a technology firm, I designed and programmed all of my systems in COBOL for a mainframe and then converted everything to a PC when this technology was feasible. Once the system was converted I successfully marketed it throughout Europe and Asia.

MY IDEAL JOB would be at a company with a technology product to market, hopefully in the securities/commodities/investment area. My job function would be to support the existing client base, bring in new clients and work with developers on existing and new customer needs/requests. I have a flexible management style that is adaptable, innovative and resourceful.

NOTE: I am geographically and financially flexible

Sincerely,

Gerald J. Saweikis

Mary C. Seymour

1251 West Henderson Street, Chicago, IL 60657

773-348-1217 mary_seymour@hotmail.com

I am submitting this letter and resume seeking your support as I pursue career opportunities in the technology, financial or consulting arenas. As you consider my credentials, please note that I am a project manager and consulting professional with broad experience that touches on staff motivation, program implementation and deployment of resources to meet client expectations. Additionally, I completed an MBA in Finance at Loyola University Chicago in May 1998, and believe that the combination of academic and practical business experience will enable me to be an immediate asset in my next role.

As a professional, I focus on maintaining a consistent management style that is accountable to the teams that I lead, the clients that I support, and the needs of my firm. At Keane Consulting Group, I help clients develop business strategies, execute the attendant action steps and make recommendations so that they achieve their corporate objectives. In addition to consulting, I have substantial experience in the financial services industry and as a registered sales assistant for Credit Suisse First Boston. In this capacity I helped clients ranging from the unsophisticated investor to the professional money manager by providing product knowledge and concise, accurate, and timely delivery of information.

Overall, my work history integrates experiences in financial services, project management, and operational consulting. Although I enjoy my role at Keane Consulting Group, I now desire another challenging opportunity that will demand my full potential. My desire is to align with an aggressive company that needs a hands-on manager with the proven talent to succeed. If you feel that my background will fit a current or prospective search that you are conducting, please contact me.

Sincerely,

Mary C. Seymour

JOHN STIGLICH
7305 W. Lake St. River Forest, IL 60305 708-488-0291

I am forwarding this letter and resume in order to pursue a senior telecommunication technology management opportunity. As you can read from the attached resume, for the past seven years, I have maintained a busy itinerary by planning and managing many corporate technology innovations and adoptions at both MCI and Montgomery Wards. With my recent position as the Regional Telecommunications Manager, I have successfully launched a number of new corporate projects that touched on reorganizing, automating and streamlining business operations at both regional and national levels. The project orientation of this experience allowed me to sharpen team leadership, executive communication and problem solving capabilities that will allow me to adapt quickly to a new corporate culture.

As an executive, I possess strong leadership values, team building insights, and decision making skills that have been tested and formed across a diverse rage of management responsibilities. The summation of my professional experience is a successful track record of developing and implementing strategic plans that affect daily systems operations for the entire corporation. I am now looking for a career opportunity that allows me to continue balancing both the human and capital aspects of business.

I would appreciate the opportunity to discuss your information technology needs and objectives at your convenience. Thank you for taking the time to review my background.

Sincerely,

John Stiglich

TAMRA THOUROT

525 North Ada, #10
Chicago, IL 60622
312-829-3171

To whom it may concern:

Enclosed is a copy of my resume outlining interior design and management skills that I have developed over the past 13 years. I've also take the liberty to include two other items - a magazine article describing my work and a marketing piece highlighting one of my designs.

Since joining The Alden Group in 1990, I've had the opportunity to help this company transition their design concepts from basic functionality to a hospitality approach by creating interiors with the ambiance of an upscale hotel. My contributions, which include innovating original design programs, have met with great success and allowed us to reach new markets. In addition to design responsibilities, are the broad-based duties that include staff coordination, vendor relations, project management as well as budget and purchasing duties which impact bottom line profitability. Over this period, I have grown as a professional and assumed increasingly demanding responsibilities. My immediate goal is to apply this valuable background in a greater design challenge.

My abilities encompass concept, design creativity, technical skills and project management. In addition, I possess strong leadership and interpersonal skills that allow me to provide effective communication and professional rapport with clients, architects, builders, and subcontractors. I am confident that your company will find my extremely high level of knowledge, motivation and enthusiasm for new challenges to be a positive contribution to the assets of your firm.

I would appreciate the opportunity to meet with you to discuss how my qualifications would be consistent with your needs. I will call your office next week to see if your schedule permits a personal interview.

Sincerely,

Tamra A. Thourot

Kevin H. Xue
5901 N. Sheridan Road Suite 9-H, Chicago, IL 60660
773-961-1543 kevinxue@hotmail.com

I am sending my resume to pursue an international business development opportunity. Since the Asian market, especially as it relates to China, is growing daily, I am hoping that you need qualified staff to help penetrate and develop the potential for you products and services in these regions. My background demonstrates a perfect blend of skills and cultural qualifications that can make me an immediate contribution to you international business team. Although I am from China where I lived until 1990, I have received an advanced education and worked in the US for the past 11 years. Over this time, I have led numerous international teams for US based corporations and Japanese companies with US operations.

As a business professional, I've worked closely with or led teams to plan and execute new media entertainment product development efforts where my emphasis has both a domestic and international focus. I am very experienced in all operational details of a modern entertainment/new media corporation. I have a firm understanding of how to find, train and motivate employees while maintaining the self-discipline and accountability to take ownership of the results.

Although I enjoy the business challenges I've met in the US, where I successfully compete with the best and biggest companies in the field, I am seeking another challenge where I will correlate personal, business and academic qualifications.

Given the opportunity, you will find me to be hard working, loyal, creative and personable. I believe it would be mutually rewarding for us to set up an interview. Once I learn more about your company, I would be happy to present you with a proposal outlining how I can help you become an even more successful company.

Sincerely yours,

Kevin H. Xue

James & Barbara Hoban

2653 N. Mildred [#3]   Chicago, Illinois 60614
(312) 883-0951

Dear Innkeeper,

We are forwarding this letter and current copies of our resumes to explore employment opportunities with your organization. We wish to convey our seriousness and sincere passion to become a husband and wife hospitality team.

Our dream is to one day operate a Bed & Breakfast or Country Inn. As you can see from the attached resume, Jim has had a career change from sales to culinary arts. After completing his certificate program at The Cooking and Hospitality Institute of Chicago, he was offered the opportunity to be part of the grand opening team of the Absinthe Cafe, a restaurant that has had phenomenal success and is currently ranked among the top 25 in Chicago. In order to help us better prepare ourselves, I also finished a hotel management class at CHIC.

Our current and past employment positions translate well to Inn keeping and property management. We feel our combined background in hospitality, sales, marketing, customer service as well as operational management experience in the restaurant/resort industries will be beneficial and allow us to become an immediate business asset. Being personable and friendly, we are confident we can help create a charming atmosphere for your guests.

If our credentials indicate that we are the team for your establishment, please call us at your convenience. Please let us know if you need any additional information. We are eagerly awaiting your reply.

Thank you,

Barbara and Jim Hoban

CHAPTER 5

NETWORKING COVER LETTERS

February 11, 2004

Terry Eagle
Leadership Gifts Director
The Cate School

Dear Terry,

I'm glad I called Ben and Ginger in December to tell them of my upcoming trip to Santa Barbara. Our phone conversation touched on what was new at Cate as well as the expansion of the development department. My admission to Ben that I desired a career change led him to suggest that I consider the Cate School. The phone conversation led to a gracious invitation to stay at his home, a long after dinner conversation and subsequent tour of The Mesa. Needless to say, my wife Carol and I were immediately drawn to the idea of becoming part of your special world.

It's amazing to find myself following in my grandfather's footsteps (he ended his career at Bradley University in the Development Office). It is also worth noting that my father was an educator as well, having taught at Avery Coonley (a Chicago area school for the gifted) and ran the department of Education at the College of DuPage for 25 years. However, his true passion was, Camp Highlands for Boys in Wisconsin, which he has directed since 1963 and attended since 1950.

It is understood that when your parents own and direct a summer camp you spend your summers there. I was exposed to countless great boys and men during this time of my life. Perhaps more than any of the younger counselors at Camp Highlands, Ben Williams was an ideal representation of what we refer to at camp as a "Highlands Man". Ben's athletic skills were remarkable, yet he was equally strong in character. To work with Ben would be a wonderful turn of events…something I never could have imagined was a possibility before December.

As for my current career, ten years ago I became an Investment Representative for Edward Jones. I have since built a successful branch office for a company that Fortune magazine ranked #1 to work for in both 2002 and 2003. My initial goal to attain upper management has been met. Life as an Investment Representative has been great because I provide counsel that improves my client's lives. Obviously, leaving Jones would require a great opportunity. My gut tells me that Cate is just what I have been hoping for and offers the intangible incentives to make the change exciting and the rewards worth the risk. My love of motivating people to do intelligent and creative things with their lives can be turned into something that has a positive impact on the Cate community.

When I began the process of writing down what I have done over the last 15 years, an exciting theme began to emerge. I ask you to read my resume carefully, not because my accomplishments are spectacular, but because the dots actually connect. All the seemingly disparate parts add up. It's incredible: you don't know where you are going at the time, but when you look back it all makes sense. It reinforces my belief in divine providence. Something special is happening. What are the chances that I would call Ben when I did…that a visit to the Mesa would ensue…that this position would be made available…that I would simultaneously start thinking about making a change in life…and that all the things I have chosen to do with my life, point to this position. I didn't even know this position existed, and yet I have intuitively done everything I could have to prepare for it. Wow!

I look forward to our upcoming explorations.

With hope and excitement,

Tim Bachmann

CONCELOR D. DAVIS

915 W. Carmen Ave., #503, Chicago, IL 60640
773-728-0015 • 773-245.4383 pgr. eyroy@aol.com

Brian Lane
Assistant Vice President
Office of the President & CEO
American Hospital Association

Dear Mr. Lane,

On the referral of a mutual friend, Robert Meier, I am soliciting your willingness to review my background for opportunities in the AHA or at one of their member affiliates.

As you can see from the resume, I've developed subject matter expertise across a broad range of business fields including account management, healthcare administration, business development, government contract administration and counseling. Since many of my roles touch on project consulting, team leadership, marketing and sales, I've learned to partner with executive management to plan and execute enterprise programs that impacted the company's bottom line. The key element that spans my entire career is the central focus on significantly improving revenues, returns on investment and profitability. Overall it is fair to say that I have a firm understanding of how to find, train and motivate team members to meet and often exceed expectations.

I realize that my amalgamated work-history touches on many business sectors, so please allow me to help you visualize what might look like a next step or a good fit. I would describe it as a position where I will be challenged to contribute professional vision, managerial seasoning, and personal integrity in order to meet the mandate of improving an entire enterprise or department as either a leader or member of a collaborative team.

Given the opportunity, your clients will find me to be hard working, loyal, creative and personable senior manager. I believe it would be mutually rewarding for us to set up an interview where I can outline how I can add value to the AHA.

Sincerely,

Councilor D. Davis

THOMAS KERN

151 Hingham Lane, Bloomingdale, IL 60108   630-351-4808

July 1, 1997

David A. Kelm
Assistant To the Governor
OFFICE OF THE GOVERNOR
2 1/2 State House
Springfield, IL 62706

    David, thank you for taking time from a busy schedule to review this information. After the Governor's Award Ceremony last month, and seriously considering your generous offer to act as a resource, I thought it would benefit you to have a copy of my resume available. Admittedly, I am not fully aware of all organizations, committees or agencies that might need a professional with my background, but an ideal situation would be a position in connection with the Illinois Law Enforcement Training and Standards Board (i.e. Police Training Specialist or a management opportunity with a Mobile Training Unit). To help you visualize possible directions, let me to summarize my career.

    With 24 years of progressive law enforcement experience under my belt, I have learned how to motivate staff, organize operations and strategically plan our mission objectives. As a professional, I focus on finding new, economical and productive ways to improve department efficiencies. As Oak Park's Training Coordinator since 1995 and as a Field Training Officer for 13 years prior to this, I have been able to deliver relevant programs that have increased professional standards of police officers, supervisors and civilians alike. I am considered to be a hands-on manager with the personality and people skills that are necessary to be accessible to both subordinates and peers.

    David, I know this is a lot of information to digest and that your schedule is full, so don't let this become a burden. Just keep it in the back of your mind and when you find time to discuss direction, avenues or possible contacts, give me a call and we can develop a strategy then.

Sincerely,

Thomas Kern

P.S.   I was able to pursue the finney denizens of the deep at Lake Shelbyville last week and thought how nice it would be to drop a bass line and brain storm together when your schedule permits.

June 15, 1998

Natalie Crossman
AMERITECH INTERNATIONAL
225 W. Randolph
Chicago, IL 60606

Dear Natalie,

I am forwarding this letter in response to the posting for a Director of Culture Change for Tele Danmark. In some ways this letter is being written not only because I so desire to transfer to an international assignment but also to honor a suggestion that Herb Hribar made to me last April. After he learned about my professional, educational and traveling experiences to France and Norway, he recommended that I continue to pursue international opportunities. As you will read, my professional experience spans a wide set of functional responsibilities that include direct marketing, operational support, account development, and new product introduction. Professionally, my objective is to continue pursuing a demanding executive career in a position that will best capitalize on these cross-functional capabilities.

Even before completing my B.S. in Marketing, and subsequently being hired by Ameritech, I desired to capitalize on extensive European travel and on two international business internships that I held in France. On an academic basis, I had the great cultural experience of participating in a high school exchange program that sent me to Oslo, Norway during the summer of 1987 and followed this up with an international educational program at Schiller University in Paris, France.   My current position with Ameritech Cellular has allowed me to sharpen organizational, client services and strategic planning skills within competitive business environments. Because of the project orientation of these assignments, my professional emphasis is to remain flexible and to focus on maximizing our resources and sales potential.

Given the opportunity, you will find that I am innovative, resourceful and capable of handling all levels of corporate responsibilities. I look forward to learning the specific qualifications that are needed to handle the role of Director of Culture. Thank you for taking the time to review my background.

Sincerely,

Michelle M. Lewis

MICHAEL E. O'CALLAGHAN
530 W. Diversey Parkway #607, Chicago, IL 60614
(312) 281-8805

June 30, 1994

Mr. Mike Cavalenes
Motorola, Inc.
600 N. U.S. Highway 45
Libertyville, IL 60048-1286

Dear Mr. Sells,

Thank you for the opportunity to present an outline of my background and experience. I am an electronics test engineer who presently seeks a position as an automated test engineer.

Bob Sauber is currently an engineering employee at Motorola at the Schaumberg facility and an acquaintance of mine. Due to my continuing interest in employment opportunities with Motorola, Bob informed me during our recent discussion, that you are a supervisor in the test equipment area. Currently I am working as a protective relay design engineer for power systems protection at Commonwealth Edison. Although I enjoy my current responsibilities, I have always intended to seek career opportunities with Motorola when the economic environment began to improve. Therefore, I would like to use this time to request an interview. This would allow me to discuss in greater detail how my background and experiences, in addition to my ability to adapt quickly to new settings, can assist you in accomplishing your organizational objectives.

I would like to thank you in advance for taking this time to review the resume.

Sincerely,

Michael O'Callaghan

Betty Dillon Regan
233 E. Wacker Dr., #1204, Chicago, IL, 60601 (312) 819-1533

Greg Saunders
General Manager
Chicago Marriott Downtown
540 N. Michigan Ave.
Chicago, IL 60611

Dear Mr. Saunders:

Recently my husband Richard spoke with you regarding my interest in current or potential opportunities in the Sales or Catering departments at the Martiott Downtown. Your reference comes at the highest level since Richard felt that your uncle Bill Burns was instrumental in his professional success.

I realize that fewer than 50% of sales representatives remain even 6 months after being hired, making managers cautious in their employment decisions. This is why I believe consistency, dedication and self-motivation are the keys for a successful sales career. I have been with the Marriott Corporation for the last 6 years learning the hospitality industry. In this time I have been demonstrating an; achievement oriented, success driven and a profit motivated personality. These are the reasons why I have been the recipient of multiple awards. With these skills and experiences I feel confident that I can become an immediate asset to the Sales or Catering departments at the Chicago Marriott Downtown.

I appreciate your time and consideration in the evaluation of this information and look forward to meeting with you for an interview.

Best regards,

Betty Dillon Regan

Chapter 5
OTHER COVER LETTERS, APPLICATIONS, PERSONAL STATEMENTS

CHAPTER 6
OTHER TYPES OF COMMUNICATION LETTERS

Jeffrey G. Caprini

1587 Burning Trail Wheaton, IL 60187 ☎ **(708) 668-0550**

Kathryn Brown
Manager MPDP,
ABBOTT LABORATORIES
Dept. 55V, Bldg. AP 34
Abbott Park, IL 60064

Dear Ms. Brown,

On the recommendation of Karl Plattner, I am forwarding this letter and copy of my resume in order to pursue a position in the MPDP program that Abbott Laboratories offers. As you can see from my background, academically I have completed a B.A. in Pre-Med at University of Illinois, and more recently, I have finished a Post Baccalaureate in Biological Sciences at DePaul University.

In order to subsidize my graduate tuition expenses, and gain practical business experience, I have taken the opportunity to manage McGees, a popular and profitable night spot here in Chicago. As a manager, my emphasis is focused on providing excellent service and building a base of customers in order to increase revenues and improve profitability. Prior to this position, I had the fortune to work as a research assistant and graduate teaching assistant at DePaul University and as a surgical aide, healthcare aide and E.R. orderly at various hospitals in Illinois. The experiences and challenges I have met during this period have taught me that hard work, innovation and determination are the keys to a successful business career.

My interest in the MPDP program centers on the desire to find a position that correlates my knowledge of biological sciences with additional training in production and manufacturing processes. After reviewing my resume I hope you will see that I can become an immediate asset to your staff.

I would appreciate the opportunity to discuss my skills and potential contributions to your company at your convenience.

Sincerely,

Jeffrey G. Caprini

DIANE JAROSZ

– spchmaker@aol.com – 7098 Hermes Lane, New Berlin, IL, 62670,
217-787-0363 home • 217-502-2765 cell

Jerald Barkmeier
P.O. Box 5598, Springfield, IL 62705
Re: Executive Director - State Farm Classic

Dear Mr. Barkmeier,

I noted the advertisement for the Executive Director position with great interest and wanted to forward this letter as a first step in qualifying for the opening. Obviously, the LPGA and State Farm have created an excellent vehicle that not only promotes two distinguished organizations, but also contributes generously to the worthy charities that benefit from the event. It would be an honor to become engaged with the mission, goals and objectives that ensure ongoing success of the State Farm Classic.

Although this is totally coincidental, it is worth noting that I have had great respect for Sandra Wheeler ever since performing with her in Springfield's Municipal Opera years ago. If I am given the opportunity to present my qualifications during an interview, I hope to demonstrate characteristics that reflect her dynamic and vivacious personality as well as the individual traits I possess that allow me to add value and perform effectively in the public arena.

I saw that you request a professional with both sales and marketing expertise, which greatly appeals to my personal expectations as I go forward in my career. Recently, working for Amtrak to promote their programs throughout Illinois as well as Milwaukee and St. Louis, I had the good pleasure of evangelizing the services offerings of this nonprofit organization. Although perception of Amtrak trends negatively in some circles, we were able to quickly turn around this view and post some of the largest gains of ridership in recent years. I firmly believe this result was a factor of practical experience gained as AVP of Speechmakers International and the multiple leadership roles I held at Horace Mann Insurance Companies. In each case, much of my focus combined sales and marketing both externally to customers as well as internally to subordinates and other managers in order to gain consensus.

It was not specifically addressed in the job announcement, but I do want to mention that I have extensive experience managing volunteers, planning events and working with executives of Fortune 500 companies as well as mid-sized organizations. As you can see from my resume, I always seek opportunity to deliver results to help my company, the colleagues I collaborate with and the customers/clients our organization supports.

I hope this brief letter offers the necessary insight to my qualifications and that you are confident to set up a meeting for us to continue evaluating whether I am a potential fit for this prestigious opportunity.

Sincerely,

Diane Jarosz

Peter Edward Mazur, *M.D.*

4804 W. Rosemont Ave.,   Chicago, IL 60646   ☎   312-283-7168

As you can see from the attached C.V., I am a graduate of the Pomeranian Academy of Medicine in Szczecin, Poland, where I received my M.D. in 1989 and maintained a strong academic standing. In 1990, I came to the U.S. to pursue the outstanding opportunities that are available in the Medical Profession and since my arrival, I have passed two of three steps of the USLME, [steps 1 by 9/93 and step 2 by 3/95].

Over the past five years, I have been working as a Mental Health Counselor for Saint Mary of Nazareth Hospital Center. At this hospital we serve as both an outpatient, and inpatient facility with 495 beds. Since beginning my tenure in 1990, I have worked on the 80 bed Inpatient Mental Health Department, with units in Medical Surgical and Intermediate Mental Health, Adolescent Psychiatry and Adult Mental Health. The typical issues that we counsel on regard symptoms of psychiatric and personality problems that include, major depression, bipolar disorder, and anxiety disorder, somatophorm disorder, as well as schizophrenia and borderline personality disorders.

Another common diagnosis with our patient population is unspecified psychosis, which generally involves issues of preexisting medical conditions, medication interactions, Parkinson's Syndrome and Alzheimer's dementia, as well as drug/alcohol overdoses that trigger psychiatric symptoms. As Counselors, we are responsible for conducting preliminary patient assessments for the staff physicians and provide individual and group therapy sessions (6-8 participants). During the group therapy, we address problems of sleep and appetite disturbances, anger, depression (e.g. hopelessness, worthlessness), suicidal tendencies, family violence, and sexual abuse. In these sessions we help determine the root causes and then provide visualization techniques, coping skills and various incentive mechanisms that offer alternative outlets to change behavior, induce positive response and resolve the entrenched psychological problems.

My attraction to the psychiatric profession is due in part to the personal challenge, and in part to the intellectual challenge. I work exceptionally well under pressure and welcome stressful or demanding situations that require critical analysis of the emergency and rational decision making for successful outcomes. I am committed to giving a 100% of my abilities in all endeavors and I know that your program requires the very best of their residents. I am trusting that your residency program will allow me to continue refining skills and developing a personal breadth of knowledge and understanding, necessary to meet the professional challenges associated with a career as a psychiatrist. I value respectable mentors and subscribe to the maxim that the practice of medicine is an ongoing and limitless learning process. I can say with complete sincerity that I enjoy the field of Psychiatry, and have found the associated responsibilities both mentally challenging and personally rewarding.

Please realize that I am dedicated to understanding human behavior and psychiatry as both a science as well as a medical specialty. I am seeking training opportunities to develop my skills and knowledge in order to build a successful career in psychiatry. I believe that the breadth of my experience will help me understand the intricate nature of people's problems and their psychological needs, not only somatic, but mental as well. I would be honored if given the opportunity to participate with your residency program.

Thank you for your attention to this matter.

Sincerely,

Peter Edward Mazur

MARCIA ROTH

1637 W. Wabansia

Chicago, IL, 60622
(312) 486-1286

January 30, 1995

NAS Confidential Reply Service,
Dept. 1CH703, 35E
Wacker Drive, Suite 1900
Chicago, IL 60601

I am forwarding this letter in response to the January 29, Chicago Tribune advertisement stating your need for a qualified Corporate Cash Manager.

As you can see from my resume, I am currently working in the Department of Trust Operations with LaSalle National Trust. Although I find the position personally rewarding and mentally challenging, it does not demand my full potential. My previous position as a Money Market Trader for CNA Insurance made me responsible for developing organizational and cash management programs. In this capacity, I controlled the short term investment needs of 40 subsidiaries with an aggregate capital base of $9.5 billion across a wide variety of financial instruments (commercial paper, T-Bills, LPC'S, etc.). From these responsibilities, I developed the instinctive capability to secure profitable trading arrangements and effectively plan and manage a large scale cash management program.

After reviewing my resume, I hope you will see that I will become an immediate asset to your organization. Thank your for taking the time to review this information.

Sincerely,

Marcia Roth

VINCE SARAC

820 W. Belle Plaine #2403   Chicago, IL 60613   Tel: (312)
244-1630

Dieter Huckestein
HILTON HOTELS CORPORTAION
9336 Civic Ctr. Dr.
Beverly Hills, CA 90209

Dear Mr. Huckestein,

Since 1990, I have been in the U.S. working for the Palmer House Hilton in Chicago. I am very interested in continuing a career with the Hilton Corporation and, have forwarded this letter and a current copy of my resume to your attention. **My primary interest is to utilize my existing international experience and knowledge of foreign cultures by pursuing assignments for Asian or Middle Eastern properties**. I would like a position that will combine my background and demonstrated experience in hospitality management, staff development and customer services.

Since starting my career in 1984, I have maintained a busy itinerary that balances my professional career with academic achievements. I now hold a B.S. in Business Administration, an A.A.S. in Hotel-Motel Management and a Diploma Certificate in Restaurant Management, additionally; I am studying for the FMP certification examination scheduled this fall. Professionally, I have handled responsibilities at the Ramada Hotels as a fine dining room manager (scheduling and supervising 40 employees) and was sent to Germany to participate in their three month management internship program. While pursuing my academic credentials, I have worked as a waiter for the Palmer House Hilton, Sheraton and Intercontinental Hotels. As you can see from the attached resume, I have been able to develop practical experience and expertise in the hospitality profession. I am now looking for a position that allows me to continue developing my staff management, customer services and organizational capabilities.

I would appreciate the opportunity to discuss my skills and potential contributions, in more detail, during an interview. Please allow me to thank you in advance for taking the time to review my background.

Sincerely,

Vince Sarac

IAIN A. SHARPE
440 N. Wabash #1711, Chicago, IL 60611   312-670-0917

Merrill Lynch
Attention Private Client Group
FC Recruiting - HP

I am submitting this letter to pursue an opportunity as a Financial Consultant within your Private Client Group. As you review my credentials, please allow me to briefly summarize specific points that should warrant your consideration.

What my background demonstrates is a unique balance of professional experience in the corporate environment as well as an entrepreneurial spirit. The fact that I have worked extensively with high net-worth clientele, have the ability to communicate persuasively and understand the characteristics of financial investment strategies will allow me to be an immediate impact to your firm. As you can see in the resume, since 1995 I have participated in a variety of positions that integrate administrative, sales, networking and staff management capabilities.

My professional history involves daily management issues that include customer relations, project support, and value added selling. The culmination of what I have learned while working at the Four Seasons along with owning my own company is to remain flexible, to always exceed expectations and to treat each client with individualized service. My public relations skills have been honed from interacting with a demanding corporate clientele. I have seen that by remaining attentive to the VIP's we serve and by quickly responding to their needs, our programs and policy goals are achieved.

I am considered to be a hands-on manager with the personality and perseverance necessary to listen and be accessible to subordinates and peers alike. In summation, these executive qualifications and management skills will allow me to be an asset to your firm.

I look forward to the opportunity to discuss in further detail your needs and my specific qualifications for this position.

Sincerely,

Iain A. Sharpe

Geographic Preferences: 1) Houston   2) Chicago   3)   New York   4) San Francisco

Romayne Badyniak
LIQUID CARBONIC R & D
3740 W. 74st.
Chicago, IL 60629

Dear Mr. Badynialc

I am forwarding this letter and the attached resume in order to pursue the entry-level position in chemical engineering you had posted at Truman College.

Because of extensive training in engineering principals, both practically and theoretically, have received at the University of Illinois at Chicago, I expect to provide immediate assistance on your engineering staff.

I have concentrated my studies on the fundamentals that include design and prototype assembly of an equilibrium separation system that involved hydraulics, liquids separation and the coordination of students to accomplish a team goal. By combining my natural enthusiasm, with leadership capabilities, that I learned while working throughout my college career, I hope to indicate to your staff that if you are looking for a team oriented employee that is also self motivated you need look no further. Because I feel that it is important to be well rounded professionally and personally I become involved in various groups at school while becoming fluent in Spanish.

The opportunity to continuously learn new skills, apply my aptitudes and to become a contributing - factor in the successful operation of an organization are the factors that motivate my efforts.

I appreciate your time and consideration in the evaluation of this material.

Sincerely,

Omar Velasquez

MARGARET A. VONESH
175 S. Oak Park Ave., Oak Park, 60302 708-848-3448

Dear Ms. Hope,

I would like to take this opportunity to apply for the job of concessions manager of the Lyric Opera. I truly enjoy my employment here at the Lyric and know that I have the knowledge, experience and leadership qualities to take on the added responsibilities of a more executive position.

Love of culture, particularly the theater, has inspired me to spend much of my life visiting the great opera houses, museums and theaters of the world. Although the arts are my passion, my resume will prove that I am eminently capable of fulfilling the duties of Food & Beverage Manager.

To work at the Chicago Lyric Opera is an inspiration for me. Attaining the promotion would be in a sense the culmination of a life's dream - to make my living contributing in some small way to the world of opera.

Sincerely,

Margaret A. Vonesh

I am soliciting search assistance as I pursue a position as: Administrator of a hospital, medical network or healthcare corporation.

Work Summary As HOSPITAL VP – Created and managed a $57 million healthcare operation consisting of –
- REMOTE MEDICAL CLINICS / EMERGENCY SERVICES / WELLNESS CENTER
- OCCUPATIONAL HEALTH / INDUSTRIAL HYGIENE / PREVENTATIVE MEDICINE
- OPTOMETRIC SERVICES / IMMUNIZATION SERVICES / SPECTACLE MANUFACTURING

Accomplished   The *Great Lakes Plan* through Senate & House Congressional committee to build a $23M central medical hospital clinic (80,000 sq/ft). This transformed a 50-year-old operation of three centers into one high-tech facility serving 400,000 patient visits annually (a 635% increase).

Management Focus - Communicate vision to the teams I lead and act as a technology catalyst to adopt medical and computer systems that enhance patient care and capture economic efficiencies. The programs I champion achieve immediate results, but are designed to stand the test of time. Overall, flexibility and persistence are the cornerstones I use to modernize infrastructures that are resistant to change.

The Bottom Line - The programs I have implemented have saved over $100 million annually for the US Navy.
If you have a search that fits my profile, please contact me at 847-735-0615 or by email at, jdbayermd@aol.com.

Sincerely,

Dr. Jon Bayer

P.S. Geographically I am completely flexible and willing to relocate.

FREDERICK YOUNG

340 S. Maple Ave., 708/386-0388, Oak Park, IL 60302 ftyoungl@sbcglobal.net

Ref Code: TD4586M
Monster.com Job Post
jobs@om5anddaystar.com
OM5 North Shore, Inc.

To whom it may concern,

I am forwarding this letter and attached resume in response to your opening for a seasoned Collections Manager.

As you can tell from the results in my resume, I've maintained a busy itinerary and managed increasingly demanding duties for two large corporations. My background combines financial management, corporate due diligence, portfolio evaluations, workouts, bankruptcy and legal support of contract administration. The central focus of my career is generating better profits from the business improvements that I design and implement.

Most recently for Alert Staffing, as Manager of Collections/Accounts Receivable, I was able to add value to the company by managing a new functional role and by creating their first turn-key collections department. This position allowed me to create programs, standards and operating procedures that had a profound impact on the financial performance of the corporation as a whole. The critical issue at Alert was to foster a collaborative environment between the executive team (CEO, COO and CFO) as well as GM's and line managers from the branches in order to reduce a significant collections imbalance.

Prior to Alert, I had the opportunity to completely revitalize AT&T Capital's approach to portfolio asset management. The end result was boosting profitability on revenues gained from equipment at the end-of-lease term. The key turning point came when I was able to prove the new system would work with my personal portfolio of business and then teach the rest of the asset managers across the other branches to follow my lead.

Overall, I am an experienced manager, troubleshooter and networker experienced with asset valuations, portfolio analysis and structuring transactions to benefit my employer. I would appreciate the opportunity to discuss the expectations of the role at your convenience. Thank you for taking the time to review my background.

Sincerely,

Fredrick Young

Chapter 7
THANK YOU LETTERS

Peter Edward Mazur, *M.D.*

4804 W. Rosemont Ave.   Chicago, IL 60646   ☏ 312-283-7168

Jane S. Lauchland, M.D.
Director, General Psychiatry Residency
KU Medical Center

3901 Rainbow Blvd
Kansas City, Kansas 66160-7341

Dear Dr. Lauchland,

Thank you for taking the time to visit with me Monday, August 21st to discuss the current residency opportunities available at Kansas University Medical Center. After spending time with you and the other faculty members, I have to admit that I am very excited about the challenges and rewards that such a position offers. It was also a pleasure to learn that your department encourages open dialog and teamwork among the medical staff. Regarding functional duties, I hope that you feel confident that my organizational and clinical experience will be appropriate for the responsibilities at hand. As well, I am very impressed with your department's stated mission and the importance that is placed on staff development and teamwork dynamics. I look forward to speaking with yourself in the near future. Thanks again for your time and interest.

Sincerely,

Peter E. Mazur

c.c.   Barry Liskow, M.D.
         Anne Guthrie, M.D.
         C. Raymond Lake, M.D., Ph.D.
         Wm. F. Gabrielli, M.D., Ph.D.
         Emad Kahn, M.D., PGY II Resident

CHRIS MILLER

1130 N. Dearborn #3105   Chicago, IL 60610 ➁ 312.944-2632

June 6, 1995

Greg Priest
Executive Vice President
BANKERS INSURANCE SERVICES, INC.
360 Central Ave.
St. Petersburg, FL 33701

Dear Greg,

Thank you for taking the time to visit with me Monday, June 5th and discuss the new products and program opportunities that your organization is planning. I am very excited about the challenges and rewards that such a position offers. My organizational and program development experience will be appropriate for the task at hand. As well, I am very impressed with your company's corporate mission and the importance that is placed on customer satisfaction. I look forward to speaking to you in the near future. Thanks again for your time and interest.

Sincerely,

Chris Miller

c.c.   Mr. Bob Menke
         Mr. David Meehan
         Mrs. Darla Bond
         Mr. Jim McFall

LAURA S. JESKE

212 West Madison Ave., Wheaton, IL 60187

July 6, 1995

Doug Metcalfe
Director of Capital Investments
AMERITECH
2000 W. Ameritech Center Drive

Dear Mr. Metcalfe,

Thank you for taking the time to visit with me Wednesday, July 5th to discuss the current opportunity that is available in your department as a manager of capital investments. After spending time with you, I have to admit that I am very excited about the challenges and rewards that such a position offers. It was also a pleasure to learn that your department encourages open dialog and teamwork. Regarding functional responsibilities, I hope that you feel confident that my organizational and program development experience will be appropriate for the task at hand. As well, I am very impressed with your company's corporate mission and the importance that is placed on staff development and internal networking. I look forward to speaking to you again in the near future. Thanks again for your time and interest.

Sincerely,

Laura S. Jeske

Letter written to the CEO of the company.

April 20, 1995

Mr. Michael T. Tomasz
Chief Executive Officer
First Industrial Realty Trust
150 North Weaker Drive
Chicago, Illinois 60606

Dear Mr. Tomasz;

Thank you very much for taking the time out of your busy schedule to talk with me about First Industrial Realty Trust and the new Director of Investor Relations position.

As I mentioned during the interview, I find the REIT industry quite fascinating. I agree with your assessment that First Industrial's stock is undervalued, and there's a great story to attract investors. The company not only has a unique, marketable niche among its immediate peer group, it is also a preferable investment compared to other REITS. I believe there are outstanding opportunities for First Industrial to educate the financial community. With increased understanding of the advantages and low risks involved with investing in FR, the stock price should rise to its fair value, decrease volatility and potentially lower the cost of capital.

After speaking with Mr. Mike Havala, I am farther convinced that you have an extremely credible management staff. In addition to my investor relation's experience, some key qualities I would bring to your team are marketing, communications and networking skills, relationship building, financial analysis, and competitive. Industry benchmarking. I have adapted quite well to my previous assignments, and am confident I could contribute very quickly to your corporate objectives.

I am very interested in the position and look forward to hearing from you. If you have any additional questions, please don't hesitate to contact me.

Sincerely,

Cindy Thorson

OMAR VELAZQUEZ

November 9, 1993

Ms. Mary Jo Para
Cost Engineer
AMOCO OIL COMPANY
Refining and Transportation
Engineering Department

Dear Ms. Para:

Thank you for taking the time last Thursday at IJIC's minority job fair to meet with me concerning potential entry level chemical engineering opportunities with Amoco Oil Company. I found your description of the position and attendant responsibilities both exciting and areas in which I am well qualified. It is fortunate that my senior design project in equilibrium-staged separation systems covered some of the basic concepts which will allow me to learn Amoco's principals quickly and become an immediate asset.

I am looking forward to continuing the interview process to learn about your needs. In the interim, if there is anything else that I can inform you about, don't hesitate to ask. Thank you again for a conversation.

Sincerely,

Omar Velazquez

Mr. Marvin Gorden
Owner/Manager
Howlett Travel/American Express

Dear Mr. Gorden,

I want to thank you for taking the time to speak with me concerning potential entry level opportunities in the travel and hospitality industry. I found your description of field and the associated responsibilities both exciting and areas in which I am well qualified. It's fortunate that Echol's Travel School covers the basic concepts, which will allow me to quickly become an immediate asset to your organization.

I am looking forward to continuing the interview process to learn about your needs. In the interim, if there is anything else that I can inform you about, don't hesitate to ask. Thank you again for an interesting conversation.

Sincerely,

Brian T. Flannery

About the Author

Robert Meier has been a practicing career coach, employment specialist and job market expert since 1991. Over that span of time he built the largest private practice in the city of Chicago, invented the first electronic resume grader and wrote "The World's Greatest Resumes", which was selected as one of the Ten-Best career books of 2005 by the L.A. Times.

Meier has been a job market expert and workforce system consultant for 20 years. Meier founded and built Chicago's largest independently owned employment consulting firm and has been consulting with local and national political leaders to bring job market efficiency to markets to reduce unemployment rates, shorten length of unemployment and improve performance of workforce investment boards across the U.S.

Meier researches a variety of job and employment macro/micro issues, including labor market dynamics as well as workforce performance & accountability. He has taught and published on a wide variety of employment issues. Meier is contracted annually by SETA (Southeastern Employment and Training Association) to train executives at 100+ workforce boards who run 1,200 Career OneStops on economic development as related to the impact of joblessness, long-term unemployment and revitalizing local economies through aggressive re-employment strategies.

Robert loves to hear from people who are using his strategies and techniques, have general career questions about how to revitalize their career path or simply want to consider using a Job Market Expert to reach their destiny for their careers. With the experience gained from helping over 4,000 clients on an individual basis, his expertise spans from the new college graduate looking to bridge the gap between their program of study and corporate American as well as senior level executives looking for the opportunities that will allow their gifts and talents to bloom.

Meier currently resides in Tampa Bay, Florida as the President of Job Market Experts.

To contact Mr. Meier – 813-838-2210
Email   Rmeier@jobmarketexpert.com